25

how to enjoy graphic design...

YEARS

of colouring in

The Paul Martin Design Company

Grateful thanks to everyone who
assisted in the production of this book
and in particular:

Paul Adams
Emma Bartholomew
Chambers Pencils
Raffaella Fletcher
Alida & Ludwig Haskins
Sharon Hicks
Steve Hobbs
Daniel Kaspar
Tim O'Kelly
Charlie Ross
Jenny Ryan

and for guest contributions by:

Quentin Blake
Alan Fletcher
Bob Gill
George Hardie
Sam Haskins
Richard Seymour

Published by
Grantchester Editions
Grantchester House
Buriton GU31 5SE
grantchester@btopenworld.com

First published 2010
© The Paul Martin Design Company Ltd
ISBN 978 0 9564733 0 1

Designed by
The Paul Martin Design Company Ltd
Printed in England by Butler Tanner &
Dennis, Fine Art Services, Caxton Road,
Frome, Somerset

To learn more about PMDC, visit us at
www.pmdc.co.uk

25 YEARS
of colouring in

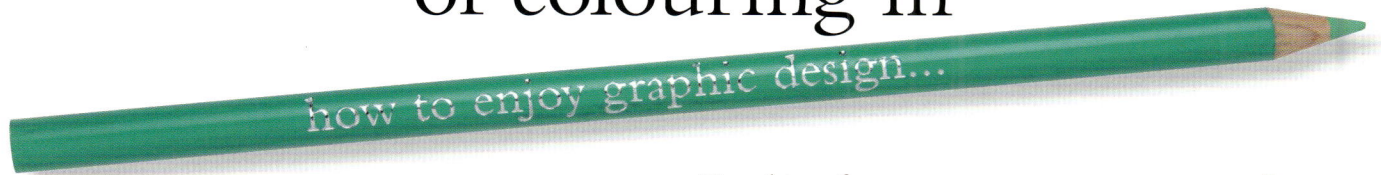

how to enjoy graphic design...

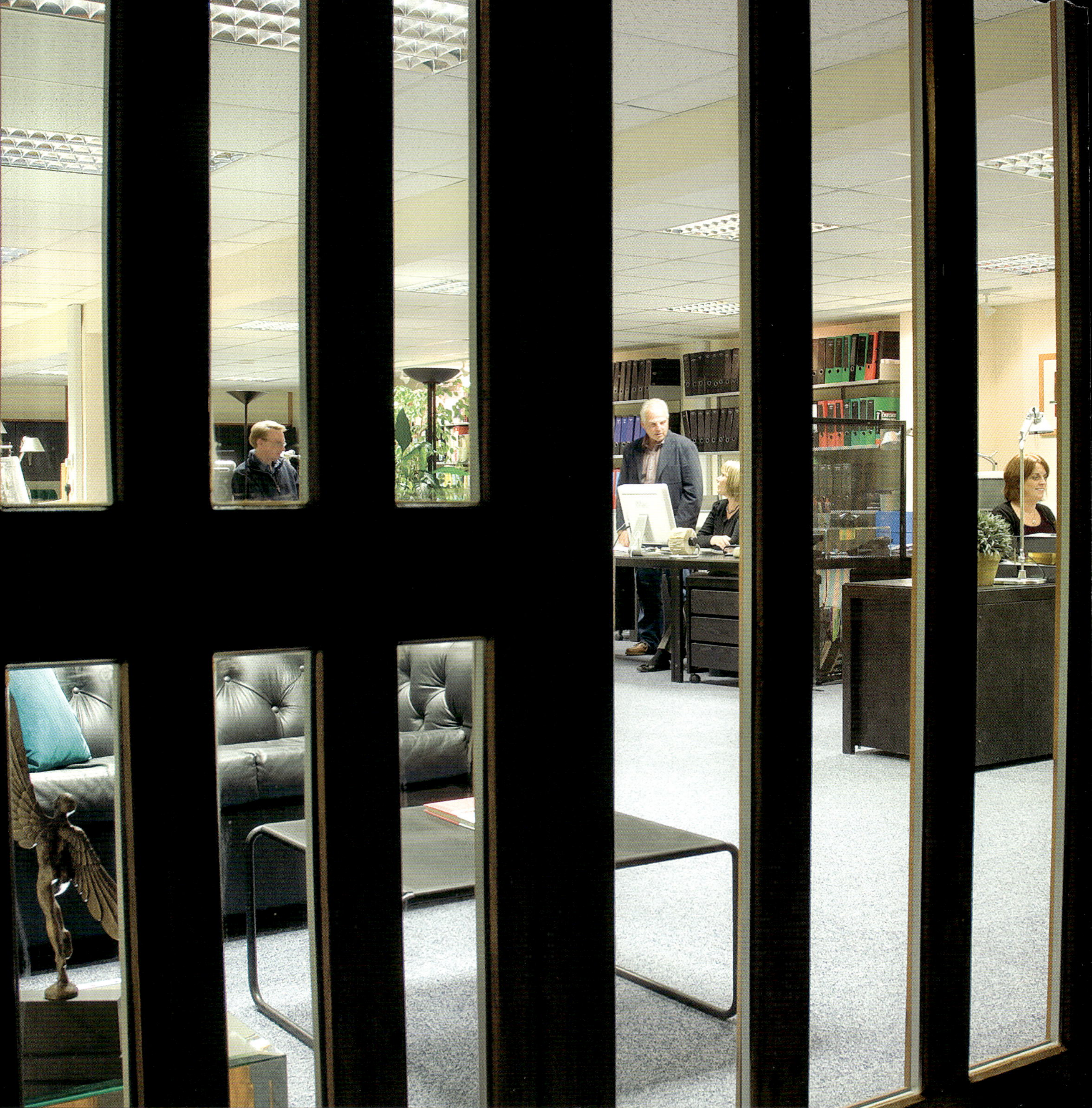

First things first...

'Colouring in' was the tongue-in-cheek term used by graphic designers to describe their vocation – one which was not regarded by many fellow professionals as being a 'real job', only something you did if you were 'good at art'. Over two and a half decades, attitudes and the technology for 'colouring in' may have changed, but the challenge for graphic designers, irrespective of the tools employed, remains the same: to be analytical, to think innovatively and to consistently employ creativity in arriving at those uniquely appropriate design solutions – whilst deriving maximum 'job satisfaction' from the whole process.

This isn't supposed to be one of those self-congratulatory 'milestone' books – more an illustration of how this particular group of designers, provincial by location rather than by nature, has reviewed and pinpointed those aspects of the business which for us has made it 'the best vocation ever' for 25 years. We've rationalised them for this book into 10 'simple steps' which ensure the continued enjoyment of the 'day job'. Illustrated by our work, we hope that they will be of interest to students of graphic design, its practitioners and its audience alike.

www.pmdc.co.uk

Mailout to announce our first website going 'on line'

6

one

Be sure to send out all the
right messages...

make every move count...

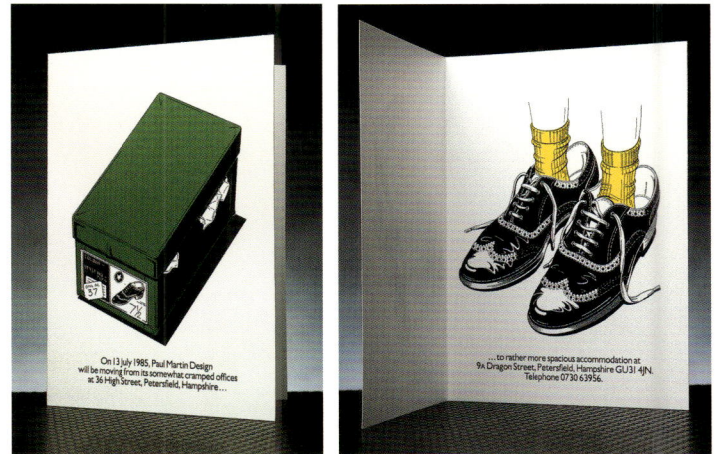

A change of address is always a good opportunity to remind clients (and potential clients) that you're capable of creative communications.

PMDC's first studio – affectionately referred to as the 'shoebox' – was soon outgrown. The observation that children enjoy a lot of extra space when aspiring to fill their parents' shoes sparked the idea for a moving card, which was eloquently interpreted by illustrator Debbie Cook.

On 13 July 1985, Paul Martin Design will be moving from its somewhat cramped offices at 36 High Street, Petersfield, Hampshire…

…to rather more spacious accommodation at 9A Dragon Street, Petersfield, Hampshire GU31 4JN. Telephone 0730 63956.

ON 30 JANUARY 1989, THE PAUL MARTIN *design* COMPANY WILL HAVE MOVED 240 FEET DOWN THE STREET TO: 32 DRAGON STREET, PETERSFIELD, HAMPSHIRE GU31 4JJ. OUR NEW *telephone* NUMBER IS 0730 65814

A second move, a short distance away, was illustrated by a '240 feet down the street' poster, shot by Phil Collins and which, as a measure of its appeal, adorned clients' and suppliers' walls long after the information had been transferred to address books and databases.

Y2K — CALVIN KLEIN

∠2000 — BRITISH HEART FOUNDATION

Y2K — HALFORDS

✳2K — THE MET OFFICE

Y2K — VEUVE CLICQUOT

whY2K? — ROYAL INSTITUTE OF PHILOSOPHERS

Y2K — THE FORESTRY COMMISSION

MILLENNIUM — THE NATIONAL HEALTH SERVICE

RSPB

LE TOUQUET / D 940 — THE FRENCH TOURIST BOARD

Y2K — HIGHWAYS AGENCY

Y3K — DOCTOR WHO FAN CLUB

Remember 'Y2K' – that abbreviation for the year 2000?
Our 'what if' takes on the millennium – a mailing which showed imagined New Year greetings from a selection of organisations

Other opportunities for what we used to term a 'mailout' are presented by events such as Christmas, anniversaries, parties, exhibitions, invitations and the dawning of a new millennium (which admittedly doesn't happen too often).

With the advent of the web and instant, electronic methods of communication, we're probably going to see an ever-decreasing amount of printed media. Not that we're stuck in the past, but it's a shame, really, as nothing purely visual can compare with holding in your hands that 'triple hit' of a well-crafted, uniquely appropriate idea, lovingly reproduced on a carefully selected paper or board.

FIND OUT HOW EFFECTIVE DESIGN CAN HELP YOUR SALES TO GROW...

1 23456789101112   1 23456789101112

BEFORE   AFTER

top left: Deserving clients all received a 'Tern of the Century'
above: Invitation to food and drink producers in the south of England to a series of marketing and design workshops

TURKEY

£ 2,512.07

Christmas fare

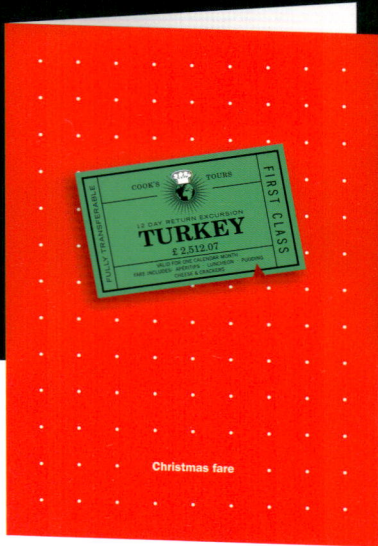

"*Now* will you find time to design the Company Christmas card?"

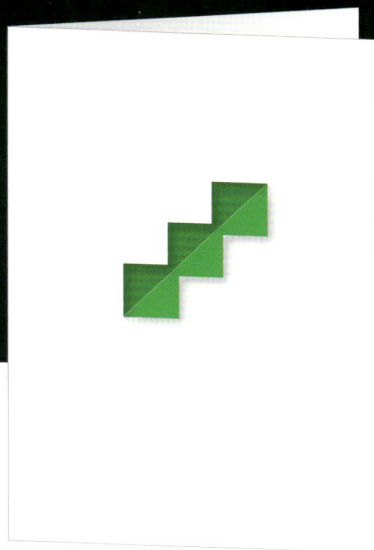

Remember the traditional Christmas card?
At 'PMDC – the early years', it was always a hotly-
contested internal brief, despite the subject of our
very first card (left).

Left hand page, top left: Homage to Belgian poster designer, Cassandre, *centre:* a 'real' ticket was hand-applied to the 'Christmas Fare' card,
right: varnished bird silhouette becomes a robin with the addition of the designer's friends, the fingerprint and chalk line.

This page, top left: Die-stamped and foil-blocked lamp (oh yes it was) for 'Christmas Wishes', *centre:* single colour inside with die-cut and fold simplicity,
right: 'Signs of the times', an idea that extended to a tag for a seasonal gift of wine *(above)*

A is for...

two

Cultivate a love of letters...

We've found it invaluable when tackling the task of creating effective identities. We'd planned to select 25 examples (1 for each year) to illustrate this notion. Trawling our archives we realised, with some surprise, that over the years we had actually 'designed our way through the alphabet'.

So, instead of 25 pieces of design, here are 26 – a kind of 'A-Z' of branding. (In one or two cases we've shown the recommended route in preference to the client's final choice. Well – it is our book!)

A

Although having the aura of an historic brand, Amber Leaf was created (and named) by PMDC in 1993

B

On the face of it, one of our less promising briefs – branding for a company offering a heating system maintenance scheme to both domestic and commercial clients. But there's always a way...

C

An elegant flight path flourish for this manufacturer of hand made beeswax candles

D

Branding 'D-vice', focal point of packaging and collateral material for Slug & Lettuce's wicked own-label energy drink

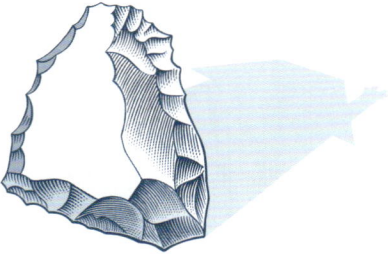

E

The EHCCI promotes dialogue and business between its members, which range from small partnerships to large corporations. The branding reflects this energetic interaction and evokes the 'wheels of industry'

F

Designed to put the competition in the shade

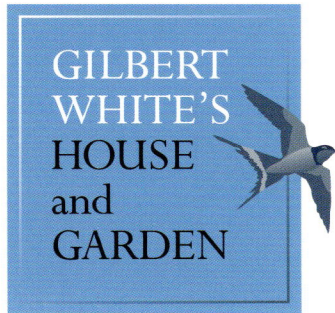

GILBERT
WHITE'S
HOUSE
and
GARDEN

hartridges
Soft Drinks

G

The house and garden of Gilbert White,
author of *The Natural History of Selborne*,
is a 'heritage of discovery in the heart of
Hampshire'

H

A fruitful combination of form and function

I

With a diamond shape and sunshine rays mirroring aspects of the Isle of Wight, we created a 'heritage' identity for this well-established island-based brewery

J

Branding for a noteworthy event

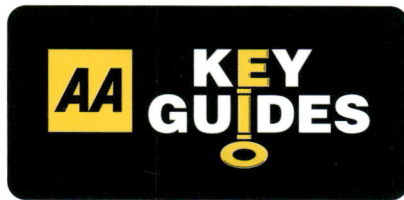

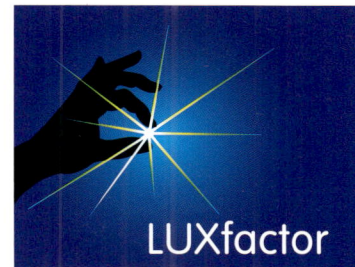

K

A memorable device unlocked the brief
for a range identity for this travel guides
series

L

Branding for a corporate and media
relations consultancy that 'reaches for the
stars'

THE MARY ROSE TRUST

BUILDING & MAINTENANCE SERVICES

M

This flowing, visual device for the Mary Rose Trust was designed to graphically reflect the ship's Tudor origins and its resurrection from a watery grave

N

In a densely populated marketplace, distinctive branding that conveys efficiency and attention to detail is the foundation on which to build a competitive advantage

open for business...

Purple Door

O

The 'O' of Oxfordshire was used to create the 'three ring' device – representing Education, Sport and Community, the three stakeholders of the partnership network

P

Purple Door opens up opportunities for the region's businesses, large or small, by promoting the University of Portsmouth's research and consultancy services and its graduate personnel

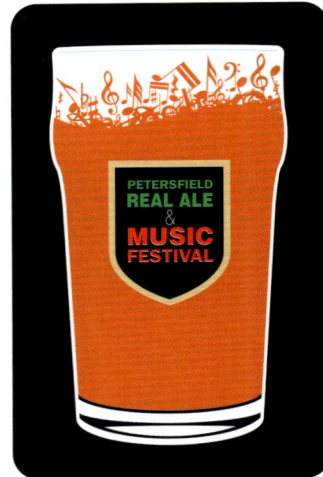

Q

Brand identity for a star performer in
interactive question and answer software

R

...is for real ale & music – always an
irresistable combination at this annual
charity event

**THE
SENSIBLE BICYCLE
COMPANY**

TITLEY AND MARR

S

Retailer that prides itself on its sound,
no-nonsense advice

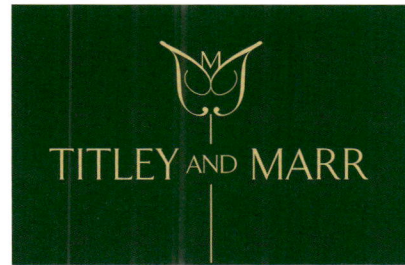

T

'T' and 'M' combine harmoniously, echoing
the floral style of this team of fabric
designers' classic creations

UK
PLATFORM
AWARDS

3VW

Verve / Vitality / Vigour

U

The prestigious UK Platform Awards, which
recognise the industry players' sometimes
stellar results, required energetic branding
and a heavyweight trophy

V

'Green' identity, ticking all the right boxes
for 3V, owner of the Meridian, Rocks and
Rasanco brands

W

Branding for a women's rugby event that
reflected and emphasised the graceful
athleticism that characterises the female
sevens game

X

A marketing consultancy specialising in
advising the food industry – 'making good
business from good food'

Petersfield **Y**outh Theatre

ZEBRA

Y

Youthful energy and exuberance reflected!

Z

Zebra Line Marking creates lines on roads,
car parks, playgrounds…

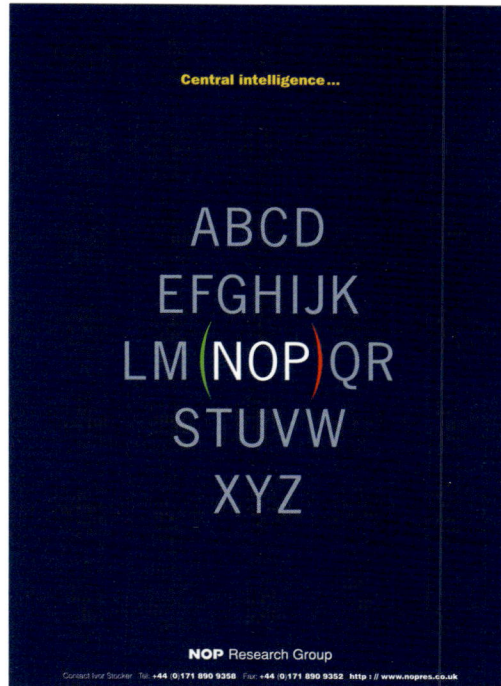

Another A–Z...

Sometimes, solutions are just there for the taking!
One of a series of business-to-business ads for the
NOP Research Group...

three

Don't get left on the shelf...

It's the constant challenge provided by packaging that helps keep us fresh. Probably the one area of graphics where you want to see your designs disappear fast. (Well no one, with the possible exception of treacle manufacturers, ever really made a successful business out of slow-moving consumer goods, did they?)

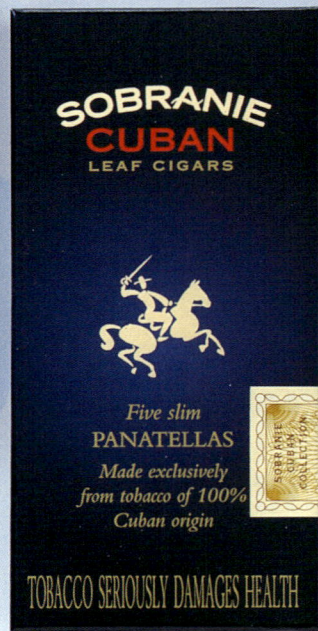

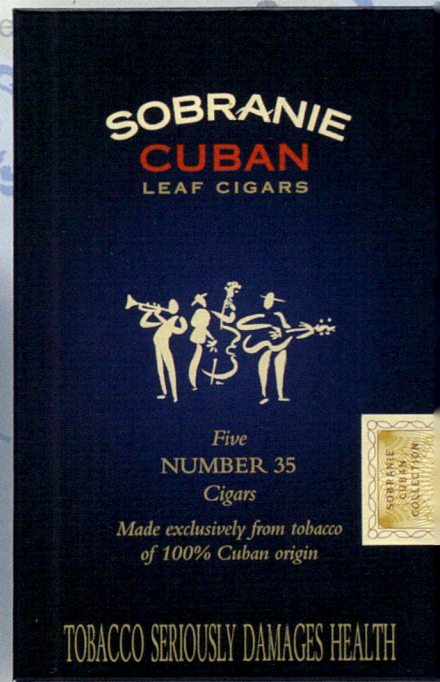

So what are the ingredients of a successful product?

We've been commissioned to provide on-shelf presence for a diverse array of products – from cigars to contact lenses, apple juice to whisky, analgesics to chocolate, candles to energy drinks – and in our experience packaging is certainly key in defining and creating brand equity.

In a nutshell, (without lapsing into 'jargonese') – to be successful you tap into the passion of the brand's owner and the character of the product and make sure that the pack radiates and reflects these qualities through its own unique 'personality'.

Simple? Not really – building brand confidence is a delicate balance of many factors, all well-documented, at length, in various publications by a variety of practitioners more analytical and articulate than us, but a few of our own designs and observations follow...

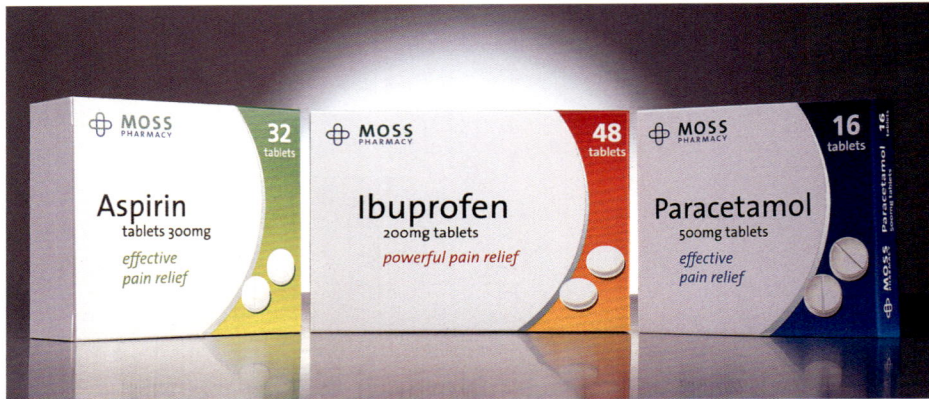

In a conservative, regulated packaging environment like pharmaceuticals, own label has to look like a credible alternative to proprietary brands, whilst for challenger brands, quality, particularly for commodity products, is paramount.

left: Analgesics from a comprehensive range of own-label packaging for Alliance Unichem's Moss Pharmacy, *right:* mixers for Hartridge's Soft Drinks

It's not every day that you get the opportunity to make use of punning packaging. *C'est Cheese* was created as one of a raft of ideas in response to a brief for concepts and packaging to stimulate the trial of different cheeses. The range researched brilliantly, but as yet, is still to see the light of day...

left: NPD concept to stimulate trial of different cheeses, *centre:* Spanish wine packaging for PLB, *right:* radical 'minimalist' design for Britain's iconic pipe tobacco

The right character of packaging can herald new opportunities and open doors. The creation of an aspirational brand identity and associated repackaging of over 100 top quality 'healthy eating' products *(above)* for the new owners of Meridian Foods, increased market share and consolidated its top three position in health food outlets whilst paving the way to listings by several of the multiple grocers.

However, one experience we had illustrates the importance of product and packaging delivering together. We were briefed (along with three or four other consultancies), to produce packaging concepts for a range of products. (No names, no pack drill). Our initial designs performed well in the first round of research, were changed little and continued to outperform all-comers in the two subsequent rounds of research. There was also every indication that, if the product was as good as the promise, a market-storming launch and huge take-up was to follow. But life is seldom as easy as a series of research documents, and we still lose sleep over what happened next. Not only was the product bland and failed to deliver the authenticity of flavour cued by the packaging, but it was marketed at a suspiciously low price-point. Credibility was shot and very few made it off the shelves, making discontinuation a natural consequence. The packaging in question (not shown here) was arguably some of the finest that we've produced to date and we're sorry that it's consigned to the waste bin of failed products.

above left: Brand identity and packaging for Meridian Foods increased market share in health food retail outlets and gained listings with major multiple grocers

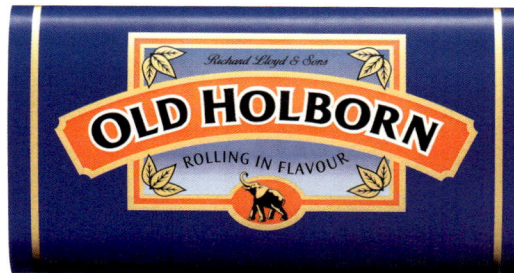

The lesson learned is that it's all very well to tap into the passion of the brand owner, the uniqueness and character of the product, and make the pack exude those qualities with a unique 'personality', but first, make doubly sure that those qualities are there.

left: Bullish treatment for 'Slug & Lettuce's' energy drink, *centre:* 'heritage' treatment for a hand-rolling classic, *right:* traditional cues for a 'halcyon days' range for Hartridges, which gained listings with Waitrose and Wetherspoons within weeks of launch

above left: Happiness is... *centre:* accessible treatment of house wines for the SFI Group,
far right: upmarket treatment for still and sparkling water reflecting the product's South Downs origins

MERLOT
2001

Caroline de Beaulieu
SELECTION

IMPORTED AND DISTRIBUTED BY THE DEMON DRINKS CO LTD
WOKING UK GU21 1JS

VIN DE PAYS D'OC
BLANC

Caroline de Beaulieu
SELECTION

IMPORTED AND DISTRIBUTED BY THE DEMON DRINKS CO LTD
WOKING UK GU21 1JS

SPARKLING

HAMBLEDON
natural spring water

275ml℮

STILL

HAMBLEDON
natural spring water

275ml℮

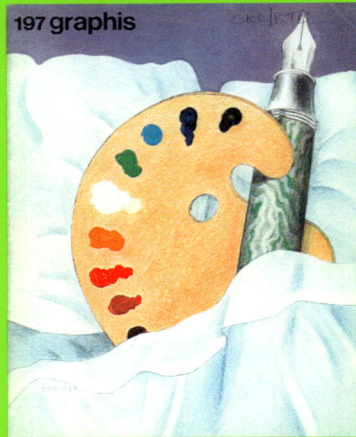

197 graphis

four

Get yourself seen in all
the right places...

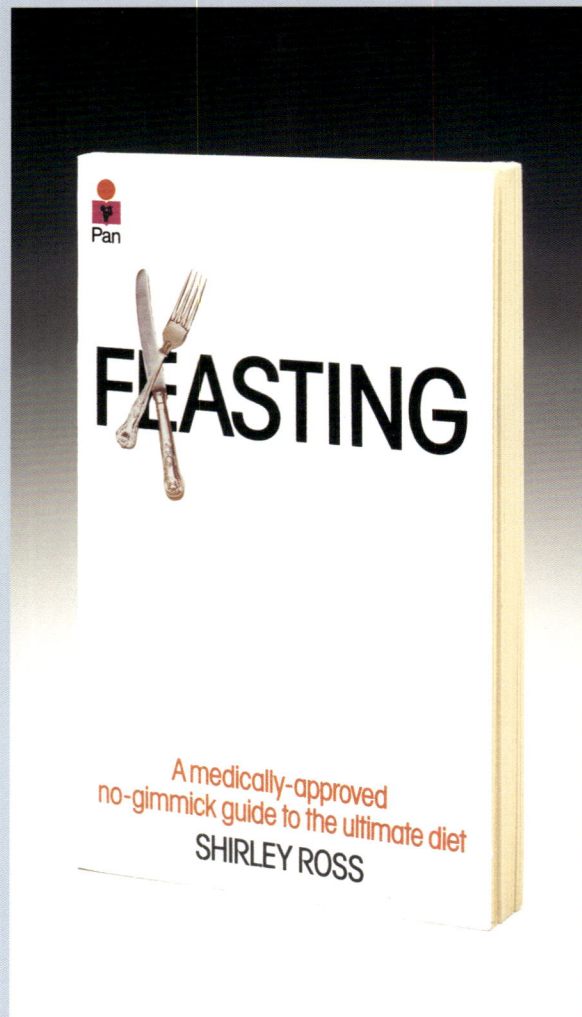

FEASTING

A medically-approved
no-gimmick guide to the ultimate diet
SHIRLEY ROSS

Pan

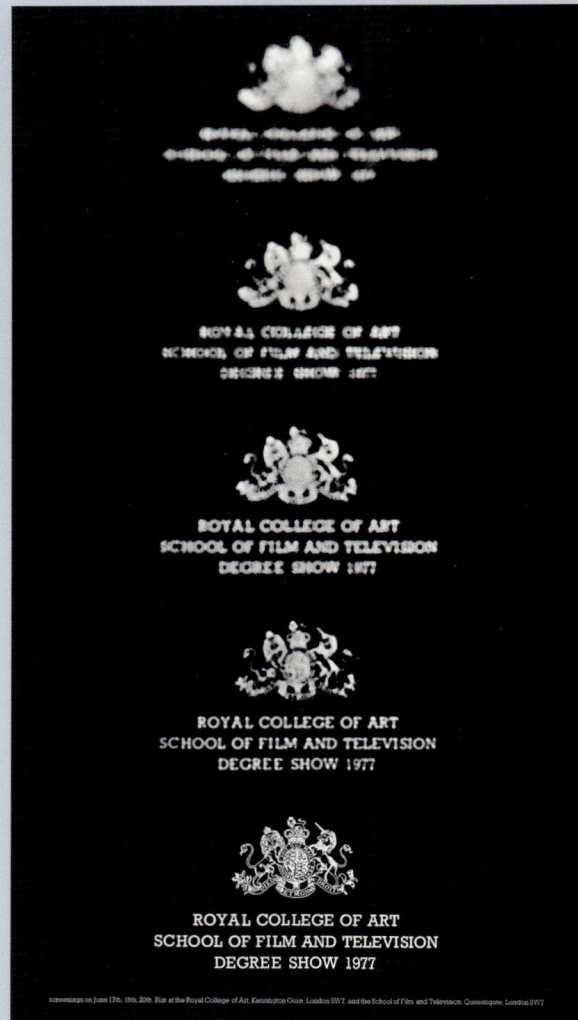

ROYAL COLLEGE OF ART
SCHOOL OF FILM AND TELEVISION
DEGREE SHOW 1977

ROYAL COLLEGE OF ART
SCHOOL OF FILM AND TELEVISION
DEGREE SHOW 1977

ROYAL COLLEGE OF ART
SCHOOL OF FILM AND TELEVISION
DEGREE SHOW 1977

screenings on June 17th, 18th, 20th, 21st at the Royal College of Art, Kensington Gore, London SW7, and the School of Film and Television, Queensgate, London SW7

A SMILE
IN THE
MIN◡

Although we're not the kind
of organisation that makes
a song and dance out of
'getting noticed', it's always good for the soul to
have work presented to a wider audience. Over the
years we've featured in a variety of award schemes
and publications such as the D&AD annual, Graphis
magazine and the design trade press. The ultimate
accolade came when Beryl McAlhone and David
Stuart of the Partners asked us to contribute to *A
Smile in the Mind* – a book about making graphics
memorable by using witty thinking. The compilation
(which contains the four pieces featured here) shows
work from over 300 designers in the USA, Britain,
Europe and Japan.

PETERSFIELD PRESENTS CHRISTMAS 2001

five

Think local...

We've found that while wooing those big city clients, the national names and global opportunities, it can be all too easy to overlook the intriguing and intellectually satisfying design challenges that are waiting on the doorstep...

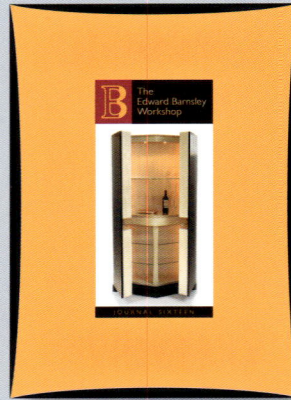

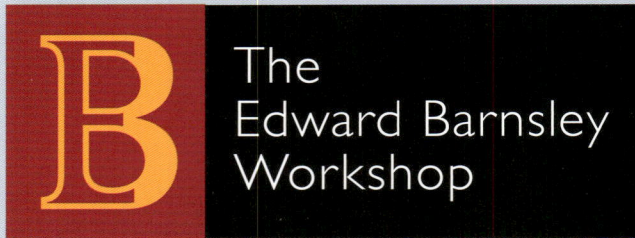

The Edward Barnsley Workshop

Edward Barnsley was a leading designer / maker of 'Arts & Crafts' furniture. His tradition lives on at his original workshop through a charity providing training for apprentices who work alongside craftsmen to create bespoke pieces of handmade furniture. PMDC's branding reflects the trademark use of inlaid woods and the benchmark precision employed in their creation of unique designs.

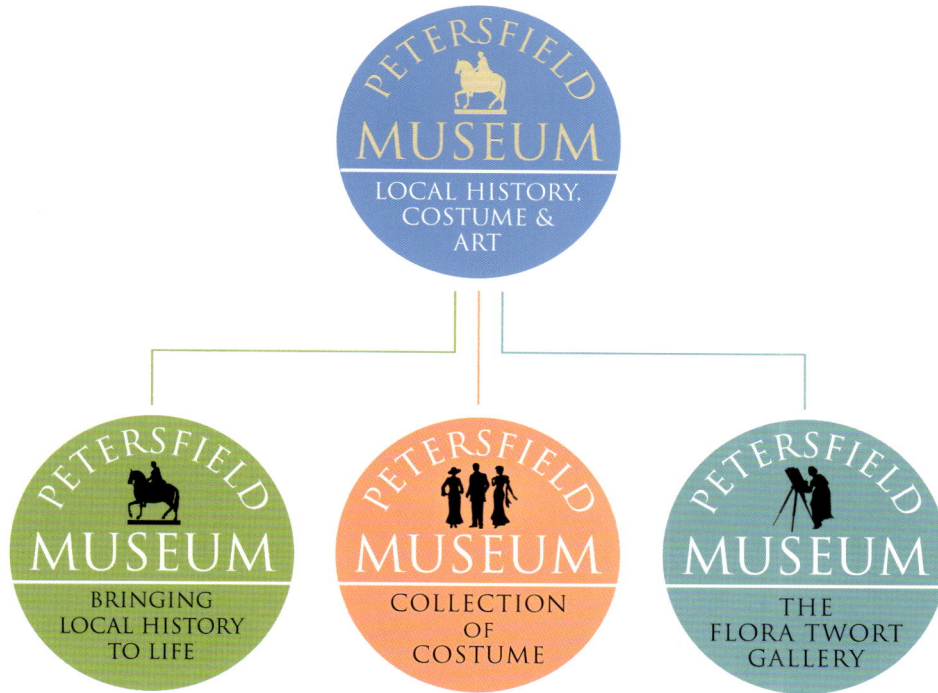

Petersfield Museum

The acquisition of a second site by Petersfield Museum prompted a Trustees' initiative to properly brand and promote the institution. Our solution to the perceived problem of two sites (actually within a stone's throw of each other), was to identify the three individual collections as 'sub-brands' under a generic Museum 'umbrella' and promote each accordingly.

Pickled egg on a dolly recipe by Vic Reeves

six

Remember that charity begins at home...

Sometimes the most intellectually rewarding and enjoyable projects are the ones that you do for free.

Jamie Oliver
THAI MARINATED STEAMED SALMON

Jo Hansford
PRAWN & ASPARAGUS RISOTTO

Alastair Hendy
WOK FRIED BASIL & CHILLI CHICKEN

John Swannell
VENISON SAUSAGES BRAISED IN RED WINE

Delia Smith
THAI GREEN CURRY with CHICKEN

Carol Vorderman
PASTA with BROCCOLI & PINENUTS

Julie Walters
COCKLES

From the sublime to the radicchio...

...was just one of our suggested titles for this celebrity cookbook. *Pickled Egg on a Doily and other Recipes* (based on Vic Reeves' contribution), along with a suitably off the wall cover, was also briefly toyed with.

One of the editors had conceived the publication as a home-produced, photocopied collection of contributed recipes, sold to raise funds to help rebuild the town of Khao Lak, the community in Thailand worst hit by the 2004 Boxing Day tsunami. It was also to serve as a memorial to some of the British people who lost their lives there.

The project gained huge momentum and grew into this celebrity-supported book. Asked to assist, PMDC provided the design and artwork on a 'pro bono' basis, calling in favours from an array of illustrators and working round the clock to meet the tight deadlines presented by a Waitrose listing and the offer of a free stand at the BBC Food & Drink Fair.

The appeal of the book is that alongside the professional celebrity chef names are an assortment of actors, singers, authors and sportsmen who contributed sometimes less than conventional recipes. ('Freddie' Flintoff's is *Fish Fingers, Chips and Beans!*)

Favourite Food from Famous Faces is in its second printing and at the time of writing has raised over £1 million for the charity, supplying facilities and sponsorship directly to the Thai community.

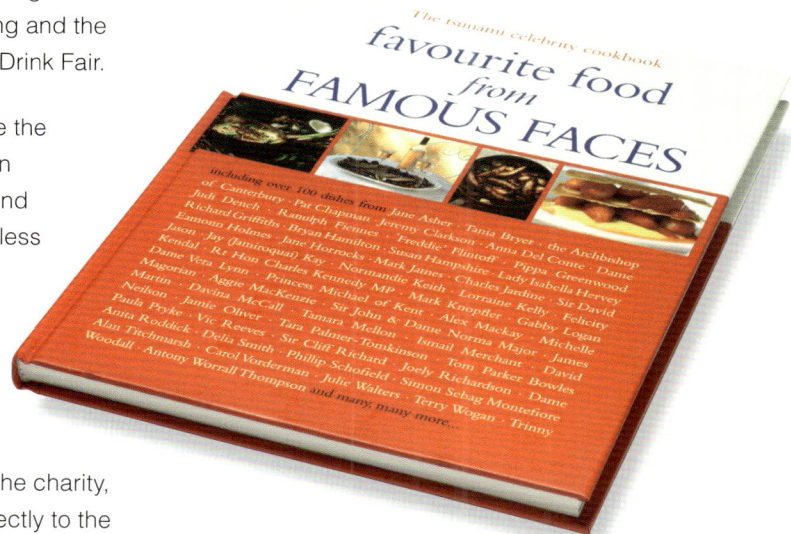

The tsunami celebrity cookbook

favourite food *from* FAMOUS FACES

Situated in the heart of Hampshire, Buriton's agriculture comprises mainly dairy and sheep farms. This led us to the 'B' branding solution *(above left)* which was required to form the basis of a campaign to raise awareness of the farmers and their contribution to the community, together with a sales push to promote the sale of their produce.

Petersfield Rugby Club was established in 1927. The branding, provided for its 75th anniversary *(below)* not only positions it as a traditional, heritage-rich club, but reflects the component sections – mini, youth, colts, senior and women – through the use of five rugby balls, which also make up its county's rose.

BREAKFAST & BRUNCH at PRFC

Get the best possible start to Sunday...

Creative opportunities are explored with PRFC promotional material

Petersfield Youth Theatre

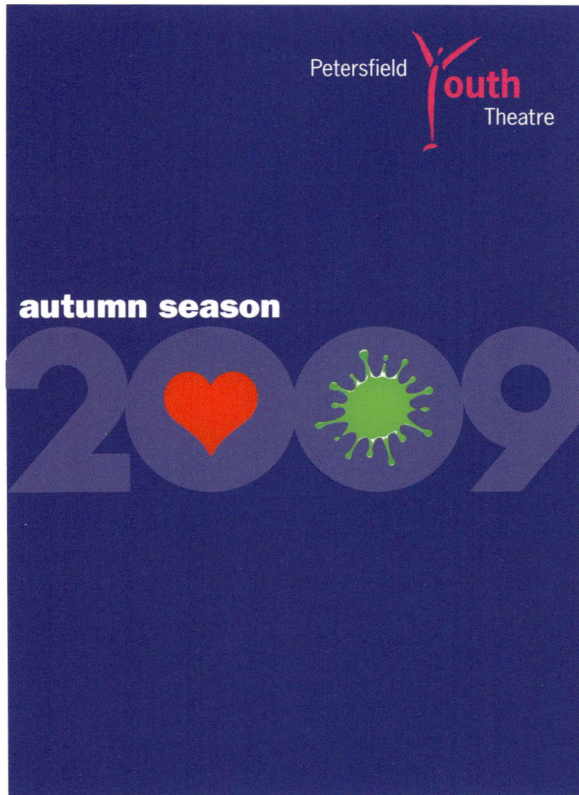

2009's heart and 'splurge' signified the productions
Carmen and *Bugsy Malone*

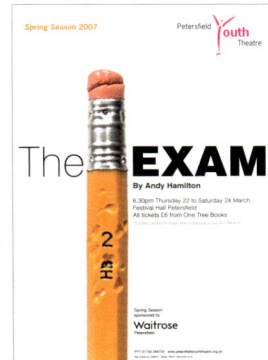

Formed in 1990, PYT provides its membership of over 300 young people aged 5–25 with the opportunity to participate in termly workshops, projects and musical productions. Some go on to greatness – Jamie Campbell Bower and Tamsin Edgerton being just two. In its role as a corporate patron, PMDC created branding a few years ago and continues to provide promotional material that underlines PYT's professional standards.

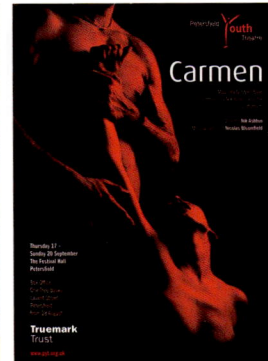

Quentin Blake explains the big idea...

seven

Learn from the Greats...

They say that you shouldn't meet your heroes, but for us it's never proved anything other than inspirational.

Head / Hand / Heart

left: National Gallery poster collage image, *centre:* poster image for International Council of Graphic Design Associations' seminar representing six speakers, *right:* one of a series of posters in which the graphic image is based on interpretation of a quotation – this one, by Ben Hecht, was also produced as a T shirt for sale at the Israel Museum of Modern Art. A curator had undergone a multiple heart bypass and naturally had an empathy with the image.

"love is a hole in the ♥ heart."

In 2003 we conceived and launched *Head / Hand / Heart* – an ongoing series of talks and exhibitions by luminaries from the world of visual arts. The title derives from the assertion by Richard Guyatt, Professor of Graphic Design at the RCA 1948 - 1979, that every piece of great art and design is a product of the head (intellect), the hand (skill) and the heart (emotion, passion). Each guest is chosen by members of PMDC as being of particular inspiration to them.

Presented in partnership with *Bedales Arts*, the talks are staged in the Bedales Olivier Theatre – itself an inspirational, award-winning building – with invited audiences comprising students, clients, business associates and friends of all ages. The accompanying exhibition is in the Bedales Gallery. Not all who attend would necessarily be aware of the speakers and their activities, or get the opportunity to see them outside of London, but all leave inspired.

This spread features *Head / Hand / Heart* illustrated by the work of Alan Fletcher, the guest at the inaugural event, *Home / Work*.

It was whilst driving back from an exhibition of Alan's work that the idea for *Head / Hand / Heart* came and we were delighted when he agreed to be its inaugural guest. His talk entertained, stimulated the mind and provoked discussion, and the eclectic nature of the work in the *Home / Work* exhibition was breathtaking.

A huge inspiration for countless students, practitioners and those who appreciate great design, Alan Fletcher made a major contribution to the profession over four decades. *Beware Wet Paint*, a book of his work, was followed by *The Art of Looking Sideways*, which deservedly continues to enjoy huge worldwide sales.

Jeremy Myerson manages to say it all: "Alan Fletcher belongs to that élite international group of designers who have transcended the conventional boundaries of their craft. He was a member of the now legendary design consultancy Fletcher Forbes Gill, and a founding partner of the international design group Pentagram. He has tackled every facet of design with a unique style and purpose, and no one else inhabits the world of ideas, of wit and ambiguity in graphic design in quite the same way. He has come to be seen as the man who took all that less-is-more, form-follows-function dogma and somehow found a way to, well, relax".

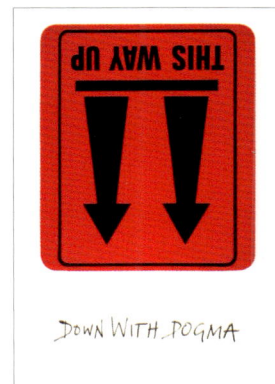

top left: 'Artistic fruit', *top right*: branding for the Victoria & Albert Museum, *centre*: 'Vagabond' pizza, *bottom right*: poster, produced for the International Design Congress
bottom left: 'Characterization'

George trained as a graphic designer at St Martin's and the Royal College of Art, and has worked for thirty-five years as a jobbing illustrator. His most public work, apart from commissions to design postage stamps, was carried out in the 1970s for and with the legendary design studio Hipgnosis. Projects for Pink Floyd and Led Zeppelin reached huge audiences. George's *Robotic Handshake* label for the shrink-wrapped *Wish You Were Here* (Pink Floyd 1975), has since been destroyed by some 16 million people worldwide, all anxious to open the package and hear the music. This image – along with the label on the record itself – is likely to remain one of George's best known drawings of hands.

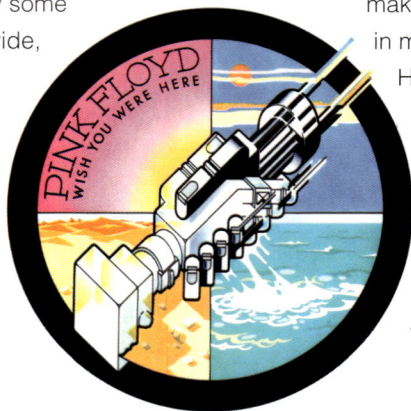

Thirty years on, and as part of a process he describes as 'going amateur', George has made a new book about hands – *Manual*. More a book of 'graphics without clients' than an artist's book, it provided the central theme for the second *Head / Hand / Heart* exhibition and talk.

As well as producing his own books, George continues to be commissioned to solve problems and make illustrations for a variety of clients in many countries (fourteen to date). His work primarily involves ideas, carefully composed and crafted into graphic art. He is a member of the *Alliance Graphique Internationale* and a Professor of Graphic Design at the University of Brighton, where he currently teaches on the MA Sequential Design / Illustration course, which is concerned with visual narratives and story telling.

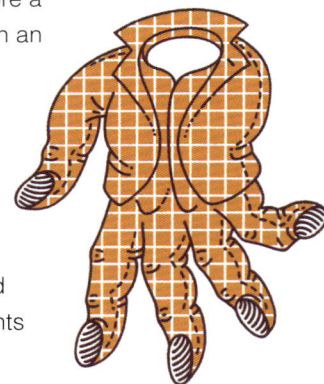

above: 'Robotic Handshake' for Pink Floyd's 'Wish You Were Here', *right*: *"Bought a suit the other day. Fits me like a glove. Four legs and one arm"*. Attributed to W.C. Fields

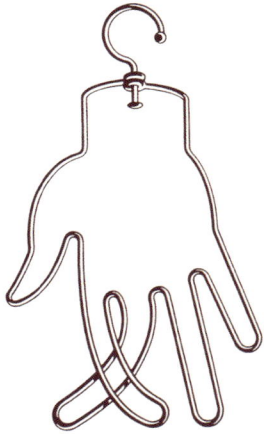

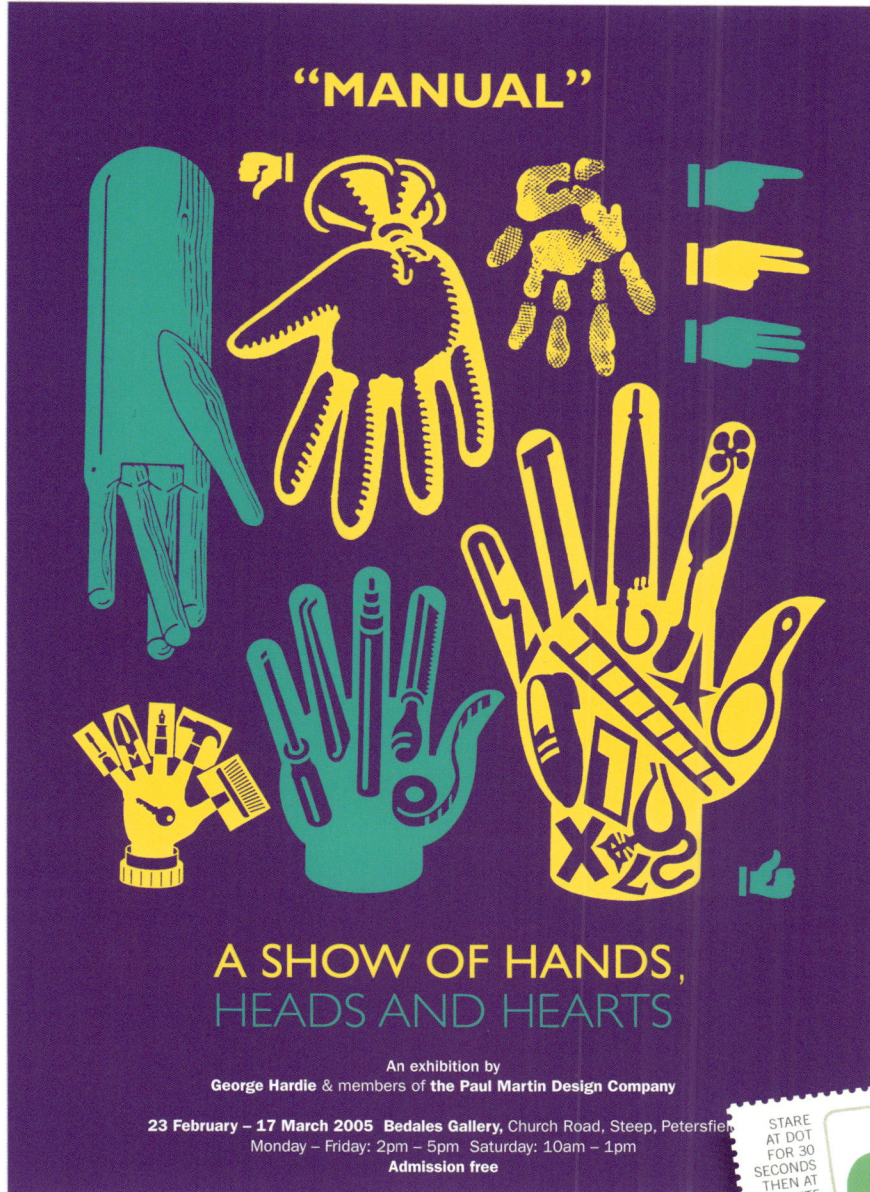

"MANUAL"

A SHOW OF HANDS,
HEADS AND HEARTS

An exhibition by
George Hardie & members of **the Paul Martin Design Company**

23 February – 17 March 2005 Bedales Gallery, Church Road, Steep, Petersfield
Monday – Friday: 2pm – 5pm Saturday: 10am – 1pm
Admission free

STARE
AT DOT
FOR 30
SECONDS
THEN AT
A WHITE
WALL

left: 'Fingers crossed', *centre*: event poster, *right*: Magic Circle anniversary stamp

Head/Hand/Heart 3 **Richard Seymour**

Richard Seymour is one of the world's best-known product designers. He has strong ideas about the role designers can, and should, play in forging a better future for us all. He also has a genuinely optimistic and positive view of the future, because he believes in the ability of the human intellect to visualise and articulate achievable answers to the problems that seem to be overwhelming us.

In his *Head / Hand / Heart* talk, entitled *Optimistic Futurism*, Richard said "It's the designer's job to fix things that don't work properly. And you start by assessing what people actually need. Why is it that over-50s are the largest group of car buyers, yet there is not a single feature – in any car, anywhere – that is designed expressly for them?"

"Design is about making life better, and about giving people emotional satisfaction when they use a product. Expense is not the issue: the electronics that dim the interior lights gradually when you close a BMW's door cost 13 pfennigs, yet this was the feature that buyers loved most when it first appeared."

Richard Seymour was one of the 100 top designers world-wide who advised Apple Computers on products and concepts for the future – the Apple Masters. "Some contemporary products, such as the iPod, seem from the outside to have happened very quickly, when in fact they were being planned years before you first saw them." he revealed. "I am working now on ideas that will change your children's lives for the better. This is why, to be a good designer, you also have to be an optimist."

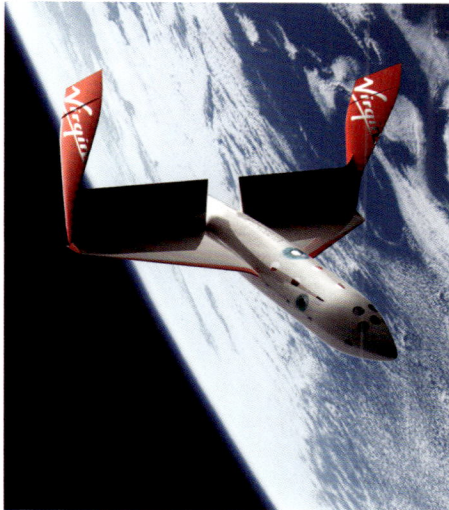

left: ENV bike, *centre:* Virgin Galactic spaceship, for which Seymour Powell designed interiors, *right:* Calor iron

Off the Page
...and on the road to St. Pancras
an exhibition of drawings and prints by

Quentin Blake

Presented by the Paul Martin Design Company and Bedales Arts
at the **Bedales Gallery** 25 February – 13 March 2009
Monday to Friday from 2 – 5pm and Saturday 10am – 1pm   Admission free
Supported by Petersfield Framing Studios

HEAD / HAND / HEART

Quentin Blake, the distinguished and much-loved artist and illustrator, was the subject of 2009's *Head / Hand / Heart*.

Most famous for his quirky, award-winning illustrations for children's books, Quentin Blake also writes and illustrates his own books for children and has illustrated classic books for adults. Since the 1990s Quentin has widened his interests to include curating shows (in, among other places, the *National Gallery*, the *British Library* and the *Musée du Petit Palais* in Paris), and illustration projects for hospitals and mental health units. In 1999, he was appointed the first ever Children's Laureate, a post designed to raise the profile of children's literature.

The exhibition *Off the Page ...and on the road to St. Pancras* focused on Quentin's increasing tendency to move beyond book illustration to creating works designed for the walls of museums, hospitals and other public places. Prints and drawings filled the gallery walls with the artist's exuberant and instantly recognisable style and the absorbing talk gave some illuminating background.

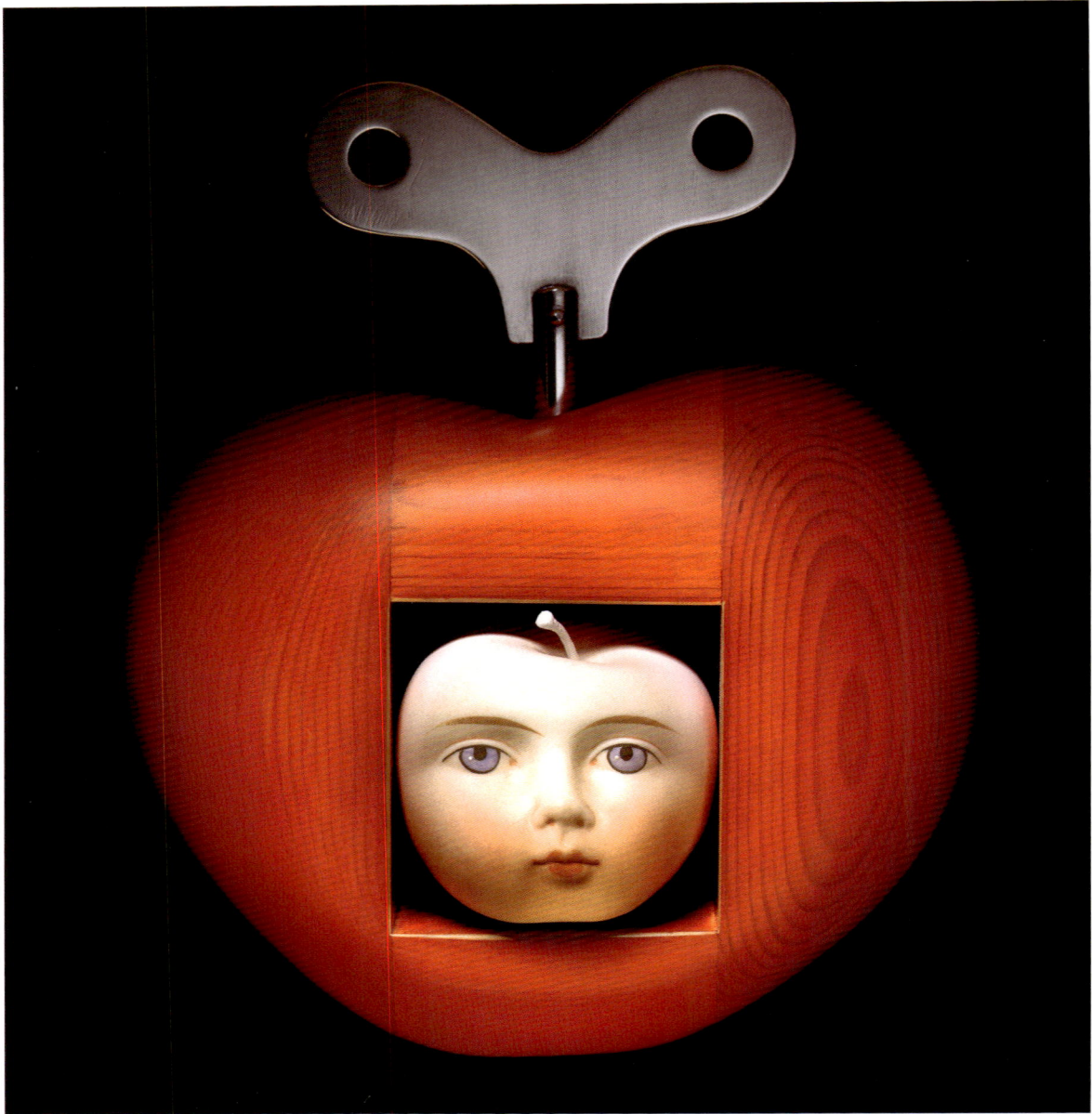

above: 'Clockwork Apple', *right hand page, top left:* 'Apple Reflection', *centre:* 'Giant Apples', *right:* 'Feathered Apple'

All photographs: concept, art direction, set construction and photography by Sam Haskins. Images on facing page from 'Fashion Etcetera' published by The Haskins Press. www.haskins.com

Sam speaks for PYT...

When legendary photographer Sam Haskins gave his *Magic Lantern Show*, an inspirational presentation of over 500 medium format slides synchronised to music, to support a fund-raising initiative by Petersfield Youth Theatre, PMDC created the promotional material *(left)*. Famous for a wide range of creative photography, especially the liberation of figure photography in the early sixties, Sam pursued a series of illustrative and graphic ideas around the theme of apples in the early '70s and returned to the subject on a few occasions later in his career. In a light-hearted tribute to these iconic photographs we created the 'speech bubble apple' especially for the event…

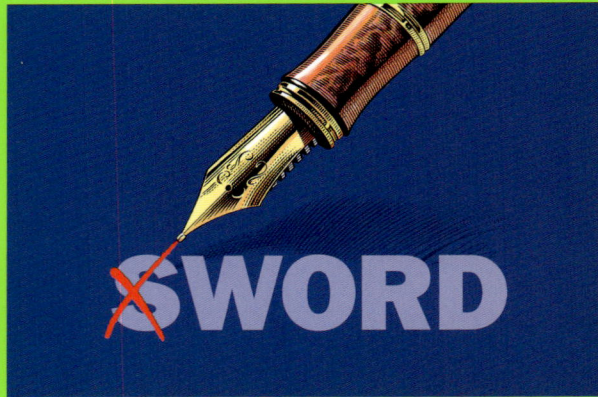

The pen is mightier than the sword – postcard souvenir of the *My Word* exhibition

eight

Make an exhibition of yourself...

Called *My Word,* this project allowed us to express ourselves outside the 'day job'. Each member of the consultancy selected a word at random and produced a piece in their own personal style for an exhibition at the Paperpoint Gallery in Covent Garden.

Jenny Ryan's word was *Happiness,* and she wrote to a variety of design luminaries asking each what happiness meant to them.

Sir Terence Conran had a list...

Happiness is a cigar called Hoyo de Monterrey Epicure No. 2 smoked in my greenhouse on a cold winter's day

Happiness is a firework display on a balmy summer's night

Happiness is a large bowl of blowsy English roses

Happiness is an applewood fire

Total happiness is a magnum of Chateau Petrus '45 drunk with one close friend

Actually, happiness is 140 beats per minute...

For George Hardie, a stalwart friend of PMDC, happiness is a spare idea...

Jenny made an uncharacteristic slip when writing to John Gorham, and mis-spelt his name. His witty riposte was a collage of a series of wrongly-addressed envelopes to him, collected over the years, with the caption *'Happiness is my name spelled right'!* (The piece, along with Sir Terence's in his beautiful, florid handwriting, is lost, sadly).

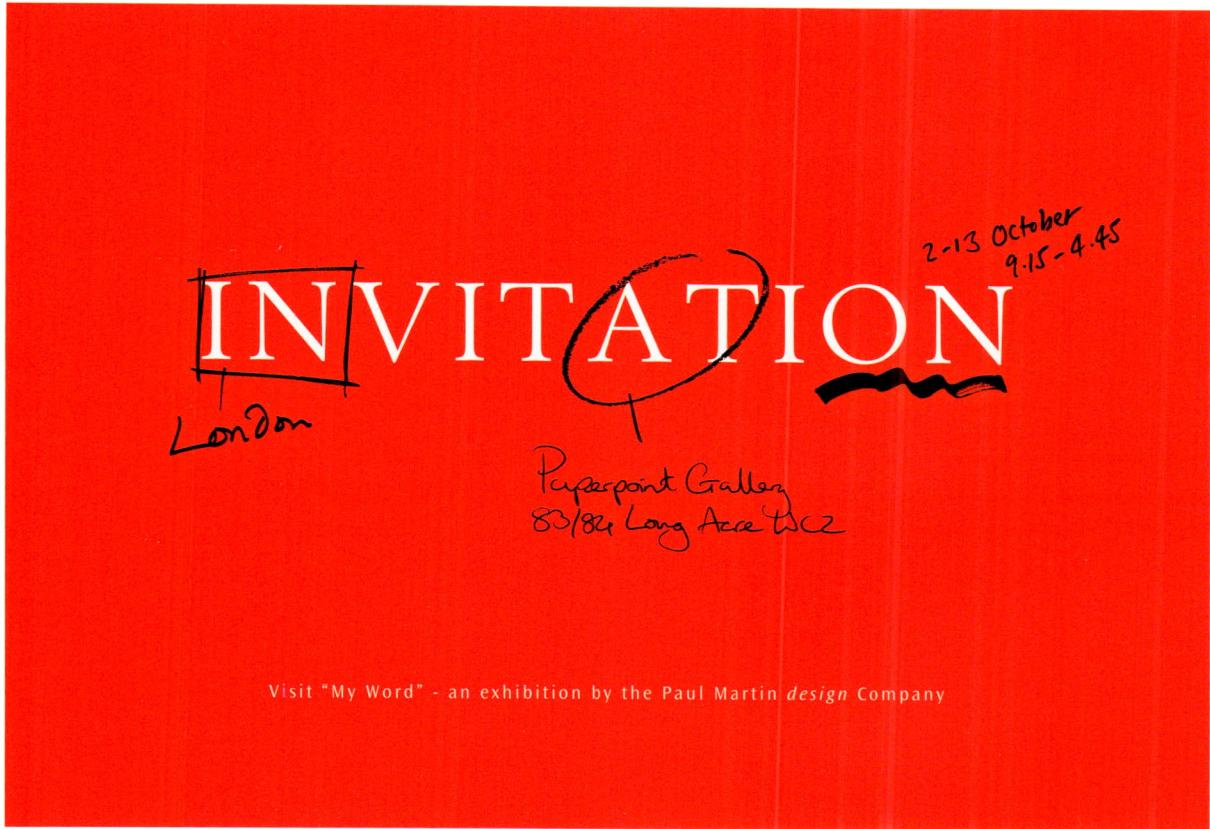

The invitation, sent out as a poster

HALF EMPTY

HALF FULL

The China anniversary...

nine

Always celebrate your
anniversaries...

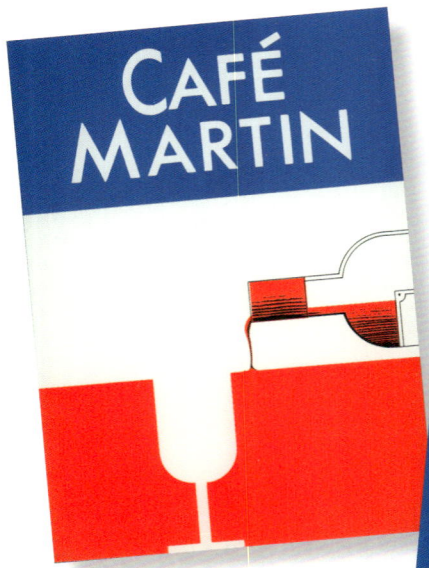

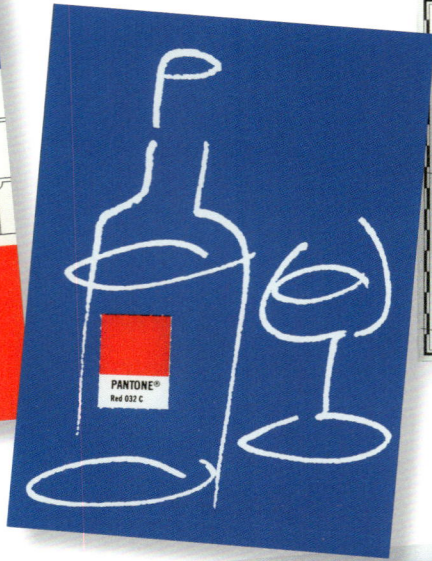

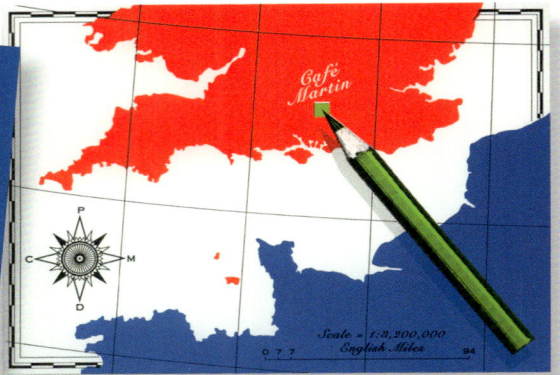

From a set of souvenir 'cartes postales' produced especially for the anniversary

When we were ten...

...we learned to seize opportunities. Serendipitously that year, the *Tour de France* bicycle race not only took in GB, but was routed past our very door. We created, and became, *Café Martin* for the day – open from dawn to dusk and enjoying a good lunch with clients, friends and suppliers just before the very swift passage of 'les cyclistes'.

Reportage photography by Michel Focard de Fontefiguieres

The 1st XV...

(years) – try celebrating with specially designed kit –
it gets over that perennial problem of what to wear to the party.

When you get to 'It was 20 years ago...'

Find a characterful barn location (a little bit older than you) and celebrate 'keeping your pencils sharp' for a second decade with a party, complete with 20 key elements, including fine food, appropriately branded drink, 20 questions (yes, every answer should be '20', but don't tell them that), a balloon race, the 'everyone's a winner draw', live music...

VINGT BLANC

VINGT ROUGE

H20 Still

Best before

31 DEC

ten

Take care of the day-to-day stuff...

Get yourself in front of existing clients (and potential ones) as many days a year as you can. We aim for 365 by producing a limited edition calendar. Each is built around a theme such as 'colour', 'numbers', 'music'. The back of each sheet carries a wealth of interesting facts or shameless trivia pertaining to the overall theme. A fun way to demonstrate creativity and establish a presence on clients' and business prospects' desks for a whole year...

HE WHO ASKS IS A FOOL FOR

fi VE

MINUTES, BUT HE WHO DOES NOT ASK IS A FOOL FOREVER

Chinese proverb

1 t
2 f
3 s
4 s
5 m
6 t
7 w
8 t
9 f
10 s
11 s
12 m
13 t
14 w
15 t
16 f

17 s 18 s 19 m 20 t 21 w 22 t 23 f 24 s 25 s 26 m 27 t 28 w 29 t 30 f 31 s may

PMDC'S calendar for **2006**

features creatures, real and imaginary...

'Nessie' makes an appearance on the **Creatures** cover in 2006...

1 m
2 t
3 w
4 t
5 f
6 s
7 s
8 m
9 t
10 w
11 t
12 f
13 s
14 s

m t w t f s s m t w t f s s m t w
15 16 17 18 19 20 21 22 23 24 25 26 27 28 29 30 31 May

Photography by our well-travelled Paul Adams

85

1	t
2	f
3	s
4	s
5	m
6	t
7	w
8	t
9	f
10	s
11	s
12	m
13	t
14	w
15	t
16	f
17	s
18	s

m	t	w	t	f	s	s	m	t	w	t	f	
19	20	21	22	23	24	25	26	27	28	29	30	June

Alan Fletcher's contribution from his 'Imaginary Menagerie'

1 t																	
2 w																	
3 t																	
4 f																	
5 s																	
6 s																	
7 m																	
8 t																	
9 w																	
10 t																	
11 f																	
12 s																	
13 s																	

m	t	w	t	f	s	s	m	t	w	t	f	s	s	m	t	w	t		
14	**15**	**16**	**17**	**18**	**19**	**20**	**21**	**22**	**23**	**24**	**25**	**26**	**27**	**28**	**29**	**30**	**31**	**August**

Spot the hidden creature in Paul Adams' Yellowstone National Park illustration.
Clue: only 1 in 10 million is born this colour...

STARS at NIGHT

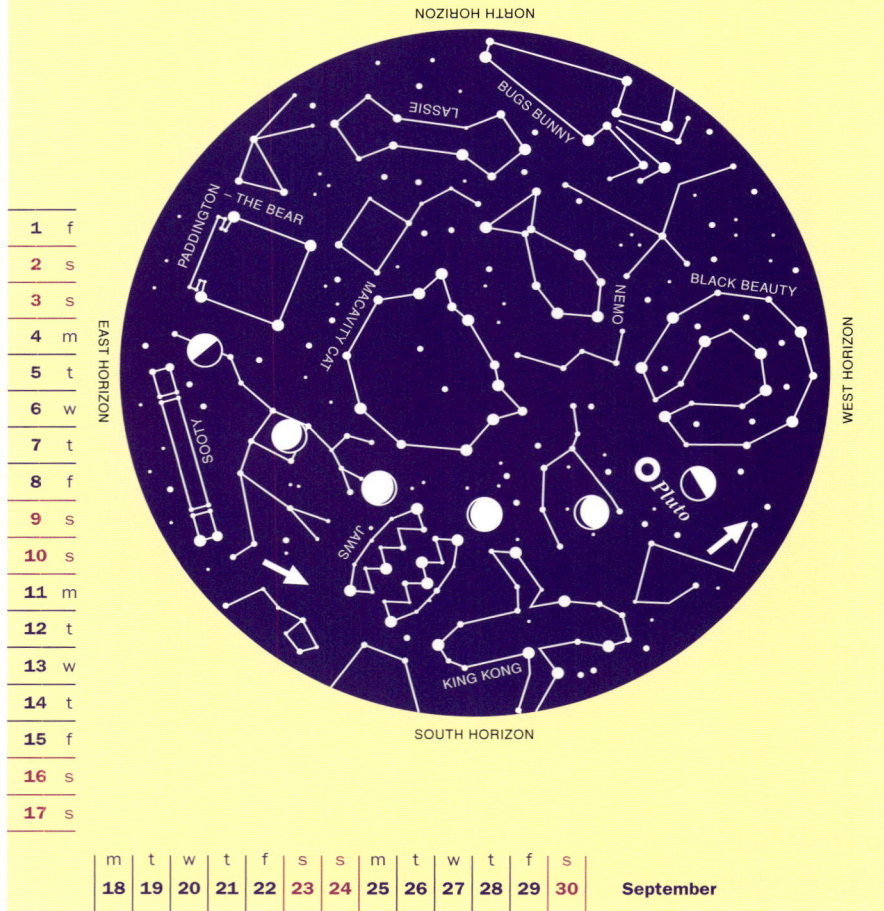

1	f
2	s
3	s
4	m
5	t
6	w
7	t
8	f
9	s
10	s
11	m
12	t
13	w
14	t
15	f
16	s
17	s

m	t	w	t	f	s	s	m	t	w	t	f	s	
18	**19**	**20**	**21**	**22**	**23**	**24**	**25**	**26**	**27**	**28**	**29**	**30**	**September**

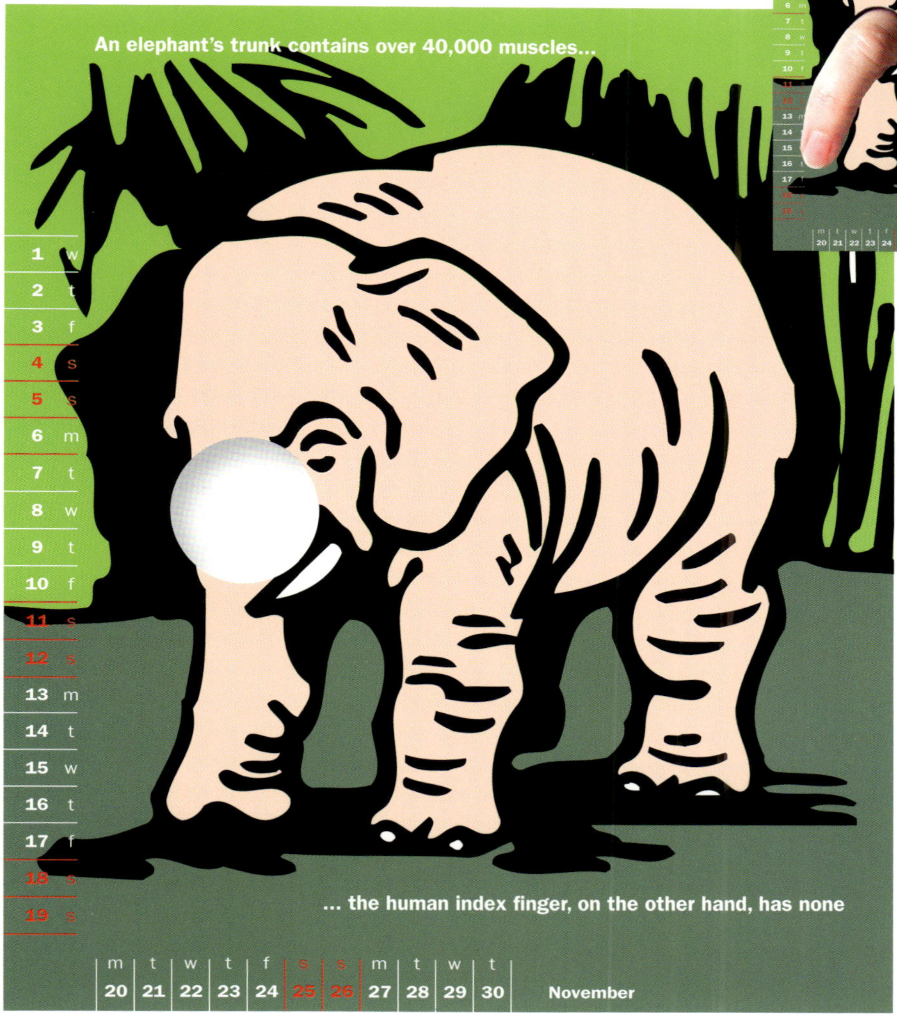

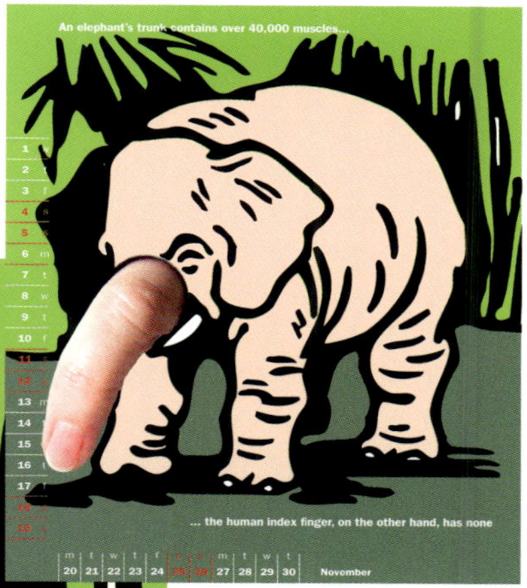

An interactive 'digital' month

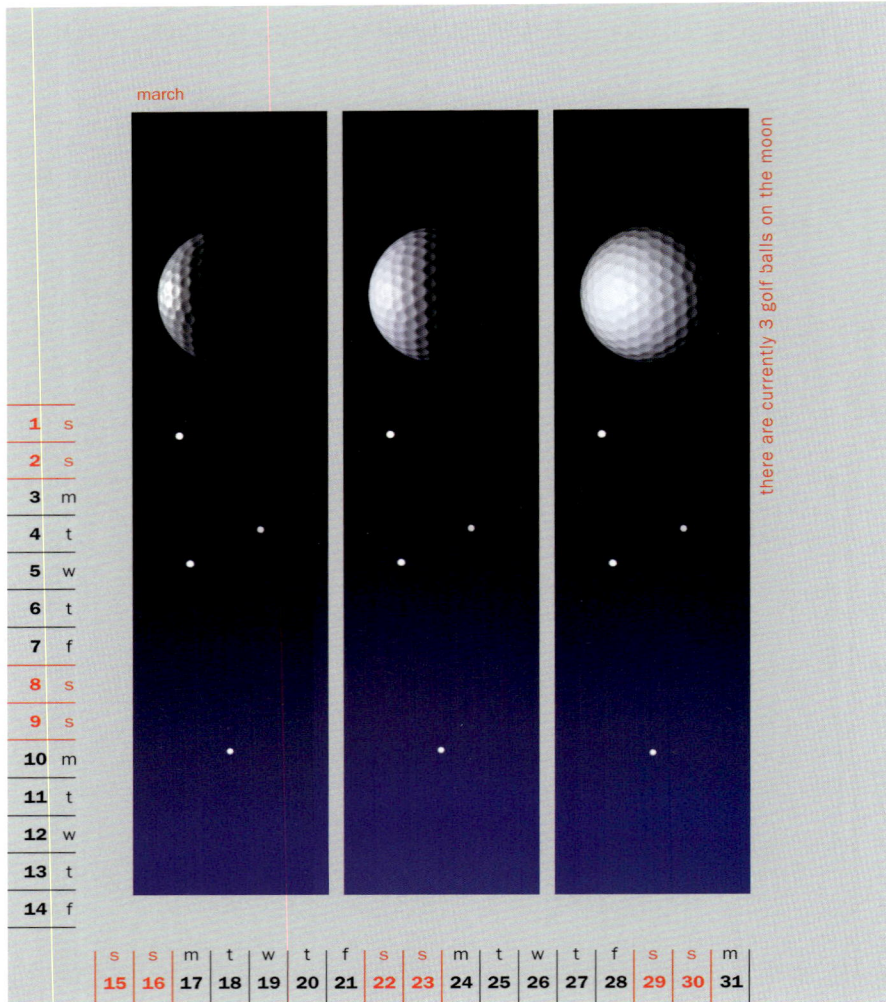

Some pages from the **Numbers** calendar...

10 **+** ADDITION 10

SUBTRACTION 10 **✕** MULTIPLICATION

1 w
2 t
3 f
4 s
5 s
6 m
7 t
8 w
9 t
10 f
11 s
12 s

10 **÷** DIVISION 10

CALCULATION **=** 10

INSTRUCTIONS:
START TOP LEFT
AND READ FROM
LEFT TO RIGHT

m	t	w	t	f	s	s	m	t	w	t	f	s	s	m	t	w	t	f
13	14	15	16	17	18	19	20	21	22	23	24	25	26	27	28	29	30	31

"I defy anyone who's ever
done a deal with Bob Maxwell
to say he didn't get a full **12** annas*
for his rupee"

Robert Maxwell 1985
*There are 16 annas to the rupee

1	m
2	t
3	w
4	t
5	f
6	s
7	s
8	m
9	t
10	w
11	t
12	f

s	s	m	t	w	t	f	s	s	m	t	w	t	f	s	s	m	t	w
13	14	15	16	17	18	19	20	21	22	23	24	25	26	27	28	29	30	31

t	f	s	s	m	t	w	t	f	s	s	m	t	w	t	f	s	s
1	2	3	4	5	6	7	8	9	10	11	12	13	14	15	16	17	18

January Hannah Pope

19	m
20	t
21	w
22	t
23	f
24	s
25	s
26	m
27	t
28	w
29	t
30	f
31	s

The **Home / Work** calendar displayed the PMDC team members' exhibits from the exhibition of the same title *(see page 60)*

April Jenny Ryan

A seamstress,
Beating out thoughts onto paper,
fashioning ideas from the fabric of words.
Home / Work - it's all the same.
It' simple enough - Home / Work.
The agony of choice; the finality of decision!
Brainstorm. Panic! Why did I go last?
She's taken my best idea.
He's taken my next - I'm lost.
My meagre imagination stripped bare,
I am the blank slate!
Quick, someone write on me!
Ideas are tossed carelessly my way -
Plain, simple, easy to execute - I can do that!
I pick them up one by one
And attempt to mould myself to their shapes.
Photography: I crawl around the garden, snapping,
Angering bees, competing with butterflies
For access to the best blooms;
But the easing of Spring is over
And the garden's dozing until the autumn blaze.
Paint next. Anyone can - look at Jackson Pollock!
I struggle to colour my imagination from a strange palette,
But my hands will not create what my brain sees;
They are speaking different languages
And I have a problem with translation.
It's not working
They squeeze and pinch.
And hand me down doubled ideas don't fit.
No! Ill-fitting hand me downs.
I want to be wearing my own ideas
I'm going to be exposed
I try again, marking out my own parameters.
I revert to words; they can be relied upon
And are easier to manipulate than paint on a canvas.
Words are my hobby horse;
The colours and shades are what I choose.
I can create my own impressions,
Be conceptual; go for realism.
Need make no allowance for bleed,
This is me: a would-be wordsmith!

1	t
2	f
3	s
4	s
5	m
6	t
7	w
8	t
9	f
10	s
11	s

m	t	w	t	f	s	s	m	t	w	t	f	s	s	m	t	w	t	f
12	13	14	15	16	17	18	19	20	21	22	23	24	25	26	27	28	29	30

Sam Farrow

1	s
2	s
3	m
4	t
5	w
6	t
7	f
8	s
9	s
10	m
11	t
12	w
13	t
14	f

s	s	m	t	w	t	f	s	s	m	t	w	t	f	s	s	m
15	**16**	**17**	**18**	**19**	**20**	**21**	**22**	**23**	**24**	**25**	**26**	**27**	**28**	**29**	**30**	**31**

'I'd rather be gardening...'

Red Admiral

1	t
2	w
3	t
4	f
5	s
6	s
7	m
8	t
9	w
10	t
11	f
12	s
13	s

m	t	w	t	f	s	s	m	t	w	t	f	s	s	m	t	w
14	15	16	17	18	19	20	21	22	23	24	25	26	27	28	29	30

1	w
2	t
3	f
4	s
5	s
6	m
7	t
8	w
9	t
10	f
11	s
12	s

m	t	w	t	f	s	s	m	t	w	t	f	s	s	m	t	w	t	f
13	14	15	16	17	18	19	20	21	22	23	24	25	26	27	28	29	30	31

Alan Fletcher's seasonal *'square, circle, triangle'* contribution

In 1987 Mathias Rust, a German
student, landed his light aircraft
in **Red** Square, Moscow
as a stunt

1	s
2	s
3	m
4	t
5	w
6	t
7	f
8	s
9	s
10	m
11	t
12	w
13	t
14	f
15	s
16	s

m	t	w	t	f	s	s	m	t	w	t	f	s	s	m	
17	18	19	20	21	22	23	24	25	26	27	28	29	30	31	**January**

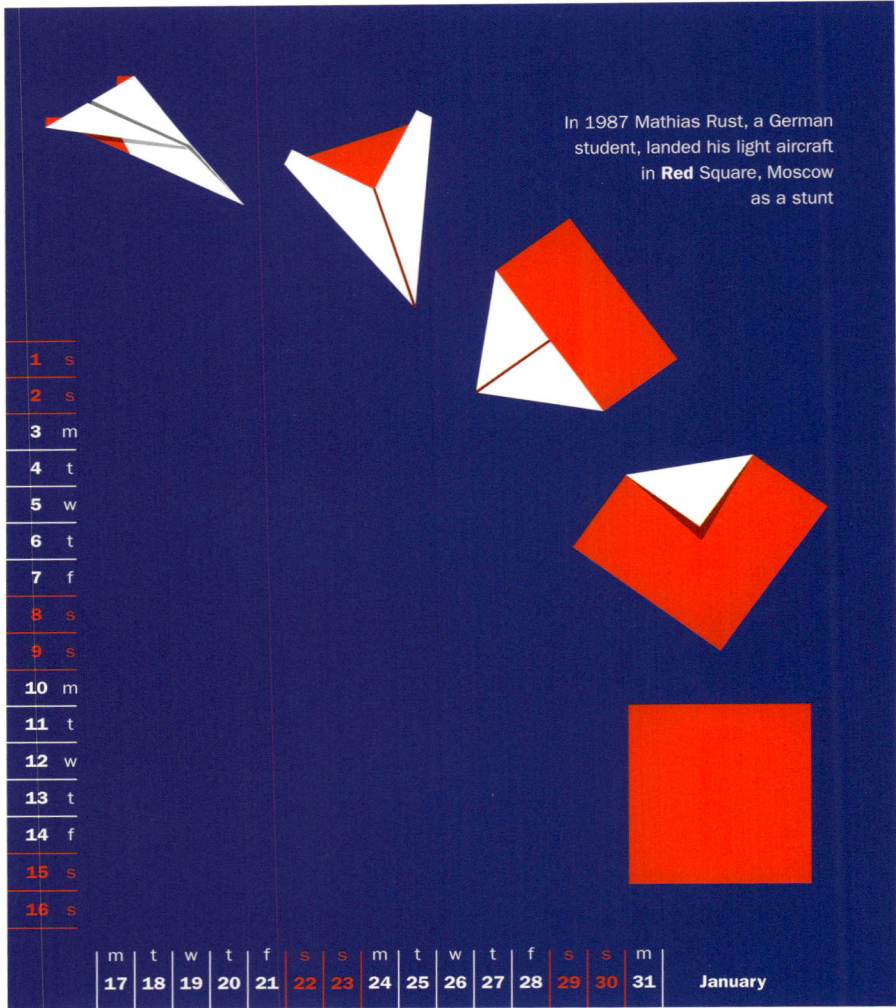

From the **Colour** calendar...

VERY LONG CAT

ONE SECOND LATER

1	t
2	w
3	t
4	f
5	s
6	s
7	m
8	t
9	w
10	t
11	f
12	s
13	s

m	t	w	t	f	s	s	m	t	w	t	f	s	s	m	
14	15	16	17	18	19	20	21	22	23	24	25	26	27	28	**February**

A black contribution from guest illustrator George Hardie

"A JAZZ MUSICIAN IS A JUGGLER WHO USES HARMONIES INSTEAD OF ORANGES"
Benny Green

CLEMENTINE #4450

1	t
2	w
3	t
4	f
5	s
6	s
7	m
8	t
9	w
10	t
11	f
12	s
13	s

m	t	w	t	f	s	s	m	t	w	t	f	s	s	m	t	w	t	
14	**15**	**16**	**17**	**18**	**19**	**20**	**21**	**22**	**23**	**24**	**25**	**26**	**27**	**28**	**29**	**30**	**31**	**March**

EVERY KIND OF BLUE

OXFORD

CAMBRIDGE

SUBTERRANEAN
HOMESICK

CHALK HILL

TOOTH

BLOOD

CORDON

IV

FLAG

CHIP

SKY

DENIM

(see over for details)

1	f
2	s
3	s
4	m
5	t
6	w
7	t
8	f
9	s
10	s
11	m
12	t
13	w
14	t
15	f
16	s
17	s

m	t	w	t	f	s	s	m	t	w	t	f	s	
18	19	20	21	22	23	24	25	26	27	28	29	30	April

101

1	s
2	m
3	t
4	w
5	t
6	f
7	s
8	s
9	m
10	t
11	w
12	t
13	f
14	s
15	s

PINK ELEPHANT

To see the pink elephant (without resorting to the demon drink)
hold the green one at arm's length and stare at it intently
for about 15 seconds. Then look at a white wall or sheet of paper,
upon which a pachyderm in a delicate shade of pink
will slowly appear...

m	t	w	t	f	s	s	m	t	w	t	f	s	s	m	t	
16	17	18	19	20	21	22	23	24	25	26	27	28	29	30	31	**May**

June	w	t	f	s	s	m	t	w	t	f	s	s
	1	2	3	4	5	6	7	8	9	10	11	12

13 m
14 t
15 w
16 t
17 f
18 s
19 s
20 m
21 t
22 w
23 t
24 f
25 s
26 s
27 m
28 t
29 w
30 t

Gold is so malleable that a piece the size of a matchbox
can be flattened into a sheet the same area as a tennis court.

From the **Food & Drink** calendar

It had seemed like a recipe for disaster. Had Berry finally bitten off more than he could chew? He certainly had a lot on his plate, having landed the plum job to make him the big cheese in the South. But then he'd always been the apple of Mr Beer's eye. And now he was due to chew the fat with the old boy. The door opened. "Come in, old man! Still keen as mustard, I see – but then you've always been worth your salt, in my opinion. And you know your onions – that's one thing that will keep you out of the soup – unlike that fellow Cox. I'm sure you share my opinion that he's a rotten apple? Never mind this 'milk of human kindness' malarkey," he continued, "Revenge is a dish best served cold. Don't want to make a meal of it, but if we could, how shall I put it, make mincemeat of him, that would be the icing on the cake for me. "Let's drink to it." the old man bellowed, proffering a glass of amber liquid. Berry drained the glass in one, noting momentarily the aftertaste of almonds. "There's something fishy about..." He never finished the sentence, but crumpled and fell like a sack of potatoes. Monty Beer smiled wryly. "As sure as eggs is eggs, you deserved that, old fruit. Do you think that I didn't know all along that you'd been cooking the books..?"

32

A novel way to back up January *(left)*

"Table for two, Mr Mondrian?"

1	f
2	s
3	s
4	m
5	t
6	w
7	t
8	f
9	s
10	s

February

m	t	w	t	f	s	s	m	t	w	t	f	s	s	m	t	w	t	f
11	12	13	14	15	16	17	18	19	20	21	22	23	24	25	26	27	28	29

meal Times

A *clair* Mrs **B** *ton* **C** *salt*

D *jon mustard* **E** *by gum!* **F** **G** *S & biscuits* **H**

I *SCREAM!* **J** *for orange* **K** **N** *pepper* **L** **M** *ntal*

'N *S' eggs* **O** *bergine* **P** *Soup* **Q** *comber* **R** *Bisto!*

S *ton* *Blumenthal* **T** *for Two* **U** *'s milk* *grey* *cheese* **V** **W**

X **Y** *t n* **Z** *Benedict*

Can you supply the missing puns?

1	s
2	s
3	m
4	t
5	w
6	t
7	f
8	s
9	s
10	m
11	t
12	w
13	t
14	f
15	s
16	s

m	t	w	t	f	s	s	m	t	w	t	f	s	s	m	
17	18	19	20	21	22	23	24	25	26	27	28	29	30	31	**March**

107

1	t
2	w
3	t
4	f
5	s
6	s
7	m
8	t
9	w
10	t
11	f
12	s
13	s

Drink cans are made from the Sahara desert!
Most aluminium cans are made from Jamaican aluminium ore or
bauxite (aluminium-rich clay). The deposits were formed from the dust
that blew from the Sahara millions of years ago.

m	t	w	t	f	s	s	m	t	w	t	f	s	s	m	t	w	
14	15	16	17	18	19	20	21	22	23	24	25	26	27	28	29	30	**April**

108

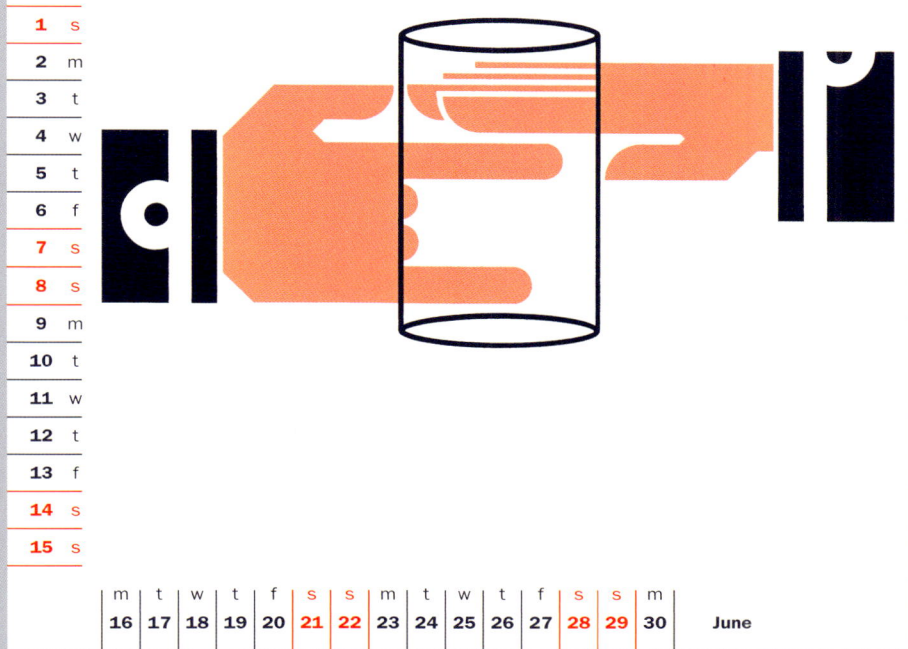

Two
fingers
of
whisky
and
four
fingers
of
water
please

1	s
2	m
3	t
4	w
5	t
6	f
7	s
8	s
9	m
10	t
11	w
12	t
13	f
14	s
15	s

m	t	w	t	f	s	s	m	t	w	t	f	s	s	m	
16	**17**	**18**	**19**	**20**	**21**	**22**	**23**	**24**	**25**	**26**	**27**	**28**	**29**	**30**	**June**

From guest illustrator George Hardie

The lady's not for churning!
Margaret Thatcher was one of
the team of chemists at J Lyons
who first developed soft ice cream

1	f
2	s
3	s
4	m
5	t
6	w
7	t
8	f
9	s
10	s
11	m
12	t
13	w
14	t
15	f
16	s
17	s

m	t	w	t	f	s	s	m	t	w	t	f	s	s	
18	19	20	21	22	23	24	25	26	27	28	29	30	31	**August**

Illustrator Graham Allen in his usual fine form...

Freddie Flintoff declares his favourite food...

		1	m
		2	t
		3	w
		4	t
		5	f
		6	s
		7	s
		8	m
		9	t
		10	w
		11	t
		12	f
		13	s
		14	s

m	t	w	t	f	s	s	m	t	w	t	f	s	s	m	t	
15	16	17	18	19	20	21	22	23	24	25	26	27	28	29	30	**September**

... fish fingers, chips and beans – illustrated by Steve Hobbs (From *Favourite Foods from Famous Faces*)

I went to a restaurant that serves 'breakfast at any time'. So I ordered French toast during the Renaissance.
Steven Wright

A spicy sausage known as *Welsh Dragon* will have to be re-named after trading standards' officers warned the manufacturer that they could face prosecution because it does not contain dragon.

The first Indian takeaway in England was the *Hindoostane Coffee House*, founded by Sake Dean Mahomed near Portman Square, London in 1809. This was nearly 50 years before the first recorded fish and chip shop, opened by Joseph Malin in the East End in 1860.

The first mobile phone call was made by Ernie Wise on 1 January 1985. The call was made from St. Catharine Docks in London to Vodafone's head office, which was situated over an Indian Restaurant in Newbury.

The average British lunch hour lasts 19 minutes and 42 seconds.

Marks & Spencer originated the sale of diagonally cut sandwiches in 1980. They were easier to stack cut that way.

How can I govern a country that has 246 varieties of cheese?
Charles de Gaulle, 1962

The Paul Martin Design Company

Alphabet soup with a Christmas message...

m	t	w	t	f	s	s	m	t	w	t	f	s	s	m	t	w	
15	16	17	18	19	20	21	22	23	24	25	26	27	28	29	30	31	**December**

1	m
2	t
3	w
4	t
5	f
6	s
7	s
8	m
9	t
10	w
11	t
12	f
13	s
14	s

(The alphabet soup has no 'L')

113

view

déja view

15 m
16 t
17 w
18 t
19 f
20 s
21 s
22 m
23 t
24 w
25 t
26 f
27 s
28 s
29 m
30 t
31 w

From the **Travel** calendar

114

Each year Britons take away with them 2,793,000 tins of baked beans...

1	t
2	f
3	s
4	s
5	m
6	t
7	w
8	t
9	f
10	s
11	s
12	m
13	t
14	w
15	t
16	f
17	s
18	s

m	t	w	t	f	s	s	m	t	w	t	f	s	
19	20	21	22	23	24	25	26	27	28	29	30	31	**March**

Journey to the centre of the Earth

Every country in the world is featured in our maze – can you find your way? Starting where indicated, use the channels between the circles of names as a pathway. You may only move from level to level where an opening between countries has not been blocked by a red dot…

1	s
2	m
3	t
4	w
5	t
6	f
7	s
8	s
9	m
10	t
11	w
12	t
13	f
14	s
15	s

m	t	w	t	f	s	s	m	t	w	t	f	s	s	m	
16	17	18	19	20	21	22	23	24	25	26	27	28	29	30	April

116

A drop in the ocean…

21.00
21.35
21.50

1	f
2	s
3	s
4	m
5	t
6	w
7	t
8	f
9	s
10	s
11	m
12	t
13	w
14	t
15	f
16	s
17	s

m	t	w	t	f	s	s	m	t	w	t	f	s	
18	19	20	21	22	23	24	25	26	27	28	29	30	June

The average journey for British commuters is 8.5 miles and takes about 45 minutes per day – that's the longest journey time in Europe.

On London's underground system, the Jubilee line is the only one that interconnects with every other line.

If you want to sail the 7 seas, they are *Antarctic, Arctic, North Atlantic, South Atlantic, Indian Ocean, North Pacific* and *South Pacific*.

However, you cannot visit the 7 wonders of the World, since only one still exists – the *Great Pyramid at Giza*. The others were *Hanging Gardens of Babylon, Statue of Zeus at Olympia, Temple of Artemis at Ephesus, Maussoleum at Halicarnassus, Colossos of Rhodes* and *Lighthouse of Alexandria*.

The furthest travelled piece of art must be Damien Hirst's 'spot' piece, created for and attached to Beagle 2, which blasted off in June 2003 attached to the European Space Agency's Mars Express spacecraft, but disappeared into a Martian crater in December 2003 after separating from the mother ship.

The Paul Martin Design Company

Signs – the universal language

ALSO AVAILABLE IN WHITE

FLAT EARTH SOCIETY

UFO VIEWPOINT

DAMIEN HIRST EXHIBITION

BERMUDA TRIANGLE

iPOD CHARGING POINT

AUSTRALIAN TOURIST INFORMATION CENTRE

WC

DRINKS PARTY

BEWARE LOUD MUSIC

PHYSIOTHERAPIST CONVENTION

WATCH OUT FOR STUNT RIDERS

1	s
2	m
3	t
4	w
5	t
6	f
7	s
8	s
9	m
10	t
11	w
12	t
13	f
14	s
15	s

m	t	w	t	f	s	s	m	t	w	t	f	s	s	m	t	
16	17	18	19	20	21	22	23	24	25	26	27	28	29	30	31	July

around the world in...

1	t
2	f
3	s
4	s
5	m
6	t
7	w
8	t
9	f
10	s
11	s
12	m
13	t
14	w
15	t
16	f
17	s
18	s

...days

m	t	w	t	f	s	s	m	t	w	t	f	
19	20	21	22	23	24	25	26	27	28	29	30	November

Face the music...

the year of **Music**

A♭ trumpet

1	s
2	m
3	t
4	w
5	t
6	f
7	s
8	s
9	m
10	t
11	w
12	t
13	f

s	s	m	t	w	t	f	s	s	m	t	w	t	f	s	s	m	t	
14	15	16	17	18	19	20	21	22	23	24	25	26	27	28	29	30	31	**March**

Jazz by Bob Gill

A contribution from the legendary Bob Gill

1	w
2	t
3	f
4	s
5	s
6	m
7	t
8	w
9	t
10	f
11	s
12	s

Guess the song (and album) title…

m	t	w	t	f	s	s	m	t	w	t	f	s	s	m	t	w	t	f	
13	14	15	16	17	18	19	20	21	22	23	24	25	26	27	28	29	30	31	July

...it was probably quite easy to guess that **Rolling Stones** classic *Brown Sugar*, but can you also work out the songs by **Blondie**, **Pink Floyd** and the **Police** suggested by the picture packs? (Also featured is the name of a hugely popular American band). See the foot of the page for the answers...

DO YOU KNOW THE WAY TO SAN JOSE?

Hangin' on the Telephone (**Blondie**), *The Wall* (**Pink Floyd**), *Walking on the Moon* (**Police**). The band is the **Eagles.**

ROCK ROUTES

1925
Show Me the Way to Go Home
Irving King

1930
Crossroads
Robert Johnson

1937
The Lambeth Walk
Noel Gay

1946
Route 66
Nat King Cole

1963
On Broadway
The Drifters

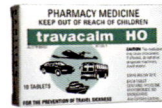
1965
Ticket to Ride
The Beatles

YOU ARE HERE
1967
My Way
Frank Sinatra

1969
Abbey Road
The Beatles

1969
The Long & Winding Road
The Beatles

1971
Stairway to Heaven
Led Zeppelin

1973
Goodbye Yellow Brick Road
Elton John

1989
Road to Hell
Chris Rea

1	s
2	s
3	m
4	t
5	w
6	t
7	f
8	s
9	s
10	m
11	t
12	w
13	t
14	f

s	s	m	t	w	t	f	s	s	m	t	w	t	f	s	s	m	
15	16	17	18	19	20	21	22	23	24	25	26	27	28	29	30	31	August

Radios by George Hardie

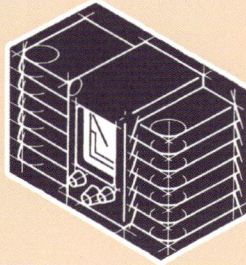

1	t																
2	w																
3	t																
4	f																
5	s																
6	s																
7	m																
8	t																
9	w																
10	t																
11	f																
12	s																
13	s																

m	t	w	t	f	s	s	m	t	w	t	f	s	s	m	t	w	
14	15	16	17	18	19	20	21	22	23	24	25	26	27	28	29	30	September

in the end...

although you'll probably find PMDC's 'simple steps' helpful, the name of the game is to make (and break) rules of your own devising. But, (and we're almost certainly preaching to the converted on this one), also recommended is extensive use of the one vital tool that hasn't changed that dramatically over 25 years – the brain.

Thanks for helping and encouraging us to be 'good at art'...

PMDC studio & administration – Paul Adams, Bianca Armstrong, Chloë Aylward, Tiffany Benn, Josh Bingley, Caroline Chandler, Andrew Cook, Roger Day, Sue Dicken, Sarah Dinham, Graham Donaldson, Jacqui Dredge, Sue Edmonds, David Farren, Sam Farrow, Tim Fuller, Sharon Hicks, Paul Hill, Steve Hobbs, Vincent Ibbs, Louise Jackson, Dean Johnson, Matthew Laakvand, Lynette Marshall, Sue McBean, Tom Northey, Christine Pack, Rachel Parker, Mike Pett, Sue Potter, Hannah Read, Denise Richardson, Jenny Ryan, Anthony Simpson, Anna Skinner, Anna Smith, Cathy Smith, Gary Spencer, Nigel Thorne, Lesley Tillotson, Michael Tribe, Andrew Turner, Simon Udal, Sarah Williams, Anna Wilson, Lavinia Winch

Illustration – Graham Allen, Phil Argent, Norman Barber, Alison Barratt, Pete Beard, Syd Brak, Debbie Cook, David Cutter, Andrew Davidson, Richard Draper, Nicky DuPays, Ian Fleming, Folio, Alastair Graham, Bob Hersey, Kevin Jenkins, John Lawrence, Linden Artists, David Loftus, Annabel Milne, Colin Newman, Michael Ogden, Peter Rauter, Bill Reid, Peter Richardson, Jeremy Sancha, Steve Seymour, Graham Simpson, Paul Slater, Lawrie Taylor, Bernard Thornton Artists, Joyce Tuhill, Ray Wiltshire

Photography – The Business, Phil Collins, Contrast Photography, Peter Dawes, Clint Eley, Michel Focard, Studio Glynde, Jeff Gorbeck, Gordon Hammond, Paul Harding, Peter Higgins, Bay Hippisley, Grantly Lynch, Monitoba, Mike Nicholson, Tim O'Flaherty, Peter Rauter, Paul Reeves, Charlie Ross, Pat Stockley

...plus some fine companies and individuals – Alchemy, Allez, Barter, Durgan & Muir, Robin Brooks, Tracey Burnett, Bruised Apple, Border Digital, John Chapman, Colourgraphic Arts, Condor, Correct Impression, Robin Dewhurst, The Embroidery Company, Fulmar, GM Print, Jane Healey, HSBC, I to Eye, Mike Imms, Tim O'Kelly, Carol Kemp, Jonathan Kirk, Leonard Gold, Chris Lee, MacDonald Oates, Mackarness & Lunt, May & Barber, Richard Mitham Associates, Moulds Builders, NJD Creative, PDQ Couriers, Perkins Slade, Petaprint, ProClean, ProPhoto, P S Financial Services, Matt Rogers, St. Richards Press, Chris Smith Modelmaking, Sussex Litho, ShutterStock, Tracey Richardson, Katherine Steadman, 2-Fruition, Town & Country Couriers, Urban Print, Bernie Vent, Web of Knowledge

and of course, the clients – The AA, Acoustic Associates, Activo, ADP Security, Agincourt Contractors, Agritek, AICC, Alert Technologies, Alliance Boots, Alliance Medical, Allied Domecq, Almus Pharmaceuticals, Alvita, American Express, And So To Bed, Artstraws, The Edward Barnsley Workshop, Barn Store, BCPC, Bedales School, Bere Dairy, Beverley Blackburn Garden Design, Blackmoor Apple Farm, Boilercare, Bongrain, Bracknell & Wokingham College, Caley's Chocolate, Cera Candela, Churcher's College, Matthew Clark, CooperVision, Cole & Mason, Contract Cleaning Direct, Creative Kids, Crop Management Services, CWC Research, Dene's Petfoods, Ditcham Park School, Dowers, East Hampshire Chamber of Commerce & Industry, EPCG, Epic Compensation, Estée Lauder, First Drinks Brands, M J Gallagher, Gallaher, Gallaher International, Garban, The Garner Group, GD Timber, Les Grandes Chais de France, Gradian, Grants of St James, Greene King, Hampshire Fare, Hampshire Wine Shippers, Hartridges Soft Drinks, The Healthcare Branding Company, Hill Farm Juices, HNW Architects, Honeywell, House of Dorchester, Ichor, ICI Garden Products, IML, The Institute of Psychoanalysis, Isabel Healthcare, JTI, Kenwood, Kingstons, The Learning Scaffold, Les Caves de Landiras, Liphook Golf Club, LuxFactor, MacMillan Press, The Mary Rose Trust, MB Games, Meridian Foods, Moss Pharmacy, Niemeyer, NKH Building, NOP Research Group, Northbrook College, Nutralife, NutriVital, One Tree Books, Oxford BioSignals, Oxfordshire Sports Partnership, Petersfield Museum, PJH Insurance, PLB, Procter & Gamble, Rizla, Rocks Organic, The Sensible Bike Company, SFI, The Studio@TPS, TechnoGraph, Titley & Marr, Torberry Feeds, Toys 'R' Us, Trevor Towner, Twinings, 2i Foods, University of Portsmouth, Vantage International, Vantage Racing, 3V, Visib, Vitacress, Warings, Waterhouse & Dodd, Gilbert White's House & Garden, Xtreme Information, Zebra

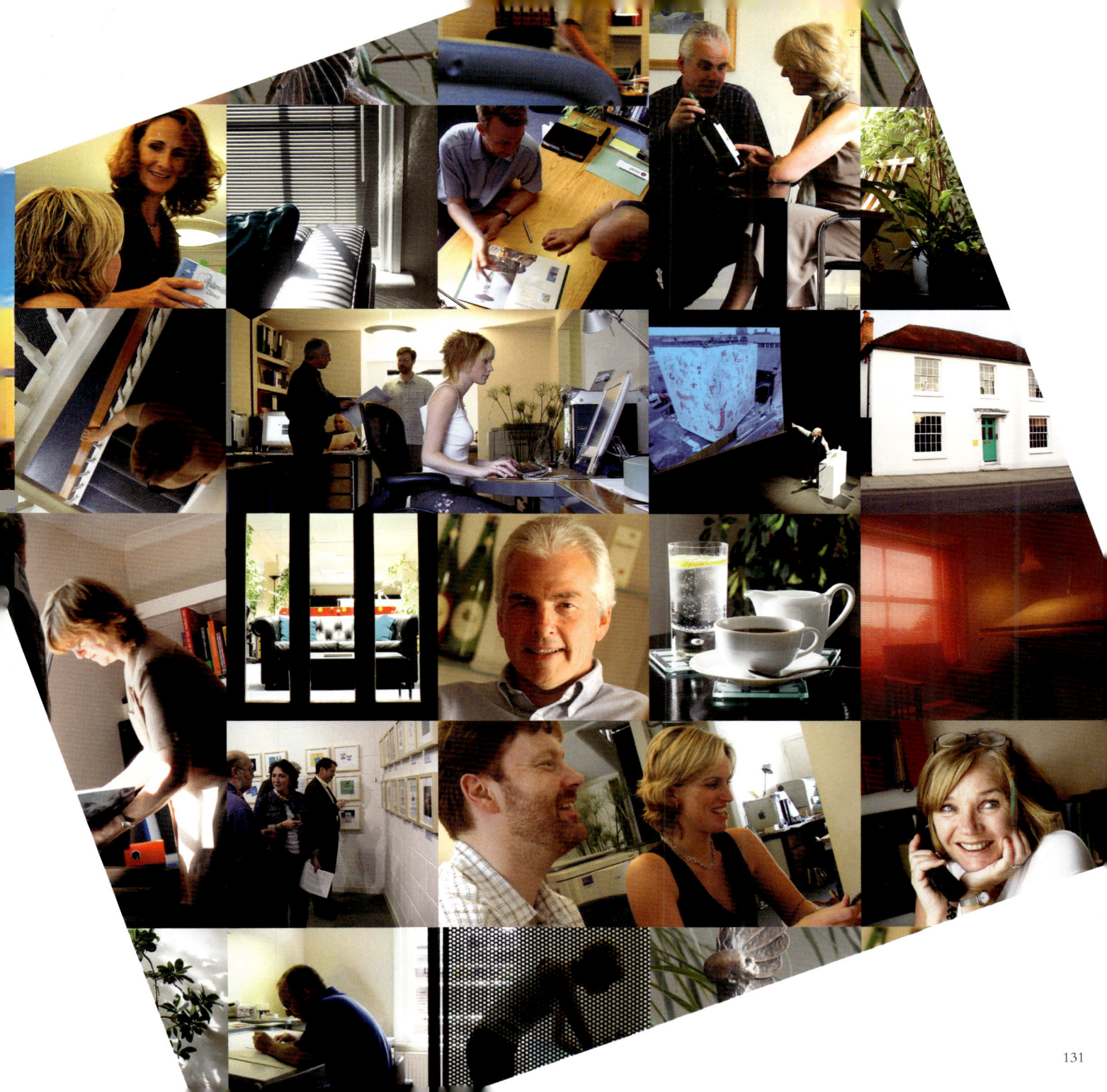

IIII̶ IIII̶ IIII̶ IIII̶ IIII̶ I